THE
SPICE
COMPANION

*The Culinary, Cosmetic
and Medicinal Uses of Spices*

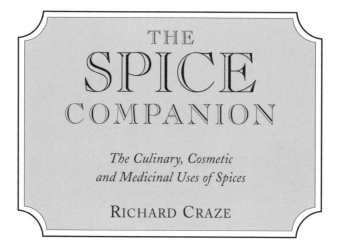

THE
SPICE
COMPANION

*The Culinary, Cosmetic
and Medicinal Uses of Spices*

RICHARD CRAZE

≡ People's Medical Society
Allentown, Pennsylvania

A QUINTET BOOK

Copyright © 1997 Quintet Publishing Limited.

First published in the United States in 1997 by the
People's Medical Society

Library of Congress Cataloging-in-Publication Data
Craze, Richard, 1950 –
The Spice Companion: the culinary, cosmetic, and medicinal uses
of spices/by Richard Craze.
p. cm.
Includes bibliographical references and index.
ISBN 1-882606-35-3
1. Spices. 2. Cookery (Spices). 3. Spices – Therapeutic use.
I. People's Medical Society (U.S.) II. Title.
TX406.C7 1997 641.3'383–dc21 97-8032 CIP

The People's Medical Society is a nonprofit consumer health organization dedicated to the principles of better, more responsive and less expensive medical care. Organized in 1983, the People's Medical Society puts previously unavailable medical information into the hands of consumers so that they can make informed decisions about their own health care. Membership in the People's Medical Society is $20 a year and includes a subscription to the *People's Medical Society Newsletter*. For information, write to the People's Medical Society, 462 Walnut Street, Allentown, PA 18102, or call 610-770-1670. This and other People's Medical Society Publications are available for quantity purchase at discount. Contact the People's Medical Society for details.

This book was designed and produced by
Quintet Publishing Limited
6 Blundell Street
London N7 9BH

1234567890 First printing, September 1997

Typeset in Great Britain by
Central Southern Typesetters, Eastbourne
Manufactured in Singapore by Eray Scan Pte Ltd.
Printed in China by Leefung-Asco Printers Ltd.

The information contained in this book is not intended to replace the advice of your medical practitioner. The author and publishers are not responsible for any adverse consequences resulting from the use or misuse of the information in this book.

CONTENTS

This book is dedicated

to the memory of

my friend Bob Lloyd

INTRODUCTION

*S*pices are, strictly speaking, the dried parts of aromatic plants—the seeds, flowers, leaves, bark or roots— although a few are used fresh. But there is something evocative about spices that goes way beyond their culinary or medicinal uses. Who can hear the words "Spice Islands" without feeling a shiver of excitement, a call of adventure and discovery? Wars were fought over spices; empires were lost in their cause. Explorers set out to find the strange and exotic lands that they came from—names that still stir the imagination—Egypt, China, Arabia, Persia, India, Greece, Zanzibar.

Some spices are worth more than precious metals and gems; both frankincense and myrrh were considered so valuable that they were included in the three gifts the Wise Men brought to the baby Jesus.

Spices are essential ingredients in any good cook's kitchen. They are also used in the manufacture of incense,

A precise definition of spices is difficult. Is garlic a spice?

oils, cosmetics, preservatives and flavorings. Their history is a fascinating and rewarding subject.

In this guide you can learn all about them—their history and cultivation, their uses and preparation. Exploring more than 50 spices from around the world, this authoritative and exhaustive guide is an illustrated directory of the essential properties of the world's most widely used and popular spices.

Star anise (Illicium verum)

But what exactly is a spice? A precise definition is difficult because some plants are regarded by some people as spices, while other people would argue that they are not. Take garlic, for instance. Is it a spice? It is certainly aromatic and spicy tasting—but it does not grow in the tropics, which is where most spices come from. The word "spice" usually means the dried seeds of certain hot aromatic plants—but what about sweet peppers? We certainly use their dried fruit in paprika, but we also use the fresh flesh—as we do for chilies. Maybe it is all in the taste. But then we would have to discount turmeric, which has little in the way of a spicy taste but nevertheless is regarded the world over as a spice; certain dishes would be lost without its brilliant yellow color. In this guide we have included all the traditional spices—as well as a few you may never have heard of but that are still regarded as important in their own countries.

MEASUREMENTS

All recipes are given in U.S. Customary units with metric measurements.

Abbreviations used are the following: tsp (teaspoon), tbsp (tablespoon), ml (mililiter), l (liter), g (gram), oz (ounce), fl oz (fluid ounce), kg (kilogram), m (meter), F (Fahrenheit), C (Celsius).

Any recipes that include a cup of ingredients refer to a standard cup holding 8 fl oz (250 ml), which is the equivalent of just under ½ pint in British Imperial measurement. Also 500 ml = 2 cups (approx.). A teaspoon is 5 ml and a tablespoon is 15 ml.

All weights are given in grams or kilos. 5 g (approx.) = 2 tsp (approx.) 10 g = 4 tsp = 20 ml. And 40 g = 5 tbsp = 80 ml.

For any recipes using eggs, medium-sized eggs are used unless otherwise specified. And a pinch or dash of spice means exactly that—the merest pinch or dash, not a handful.

Oven temperatures are not usually given because they can vary so much. However, we would recommend a moderate heat of 350°–375°F (180°–190°C).

CAUTION
Any medicinal uses are given purely for information. Any conditions that require medical attention should be referred to a qualified medical doctor. No attempt should be made to treat any serious conditions at home.

THE SPICE DIRECTORY

The directory contains the most important, common, exotic and unusual spices from around the world. It includes well-known and commonly used spices such as black pepper, mustard and caraway as well as not-so-well-known ones such as java galangal and asafetida. The directory for each spice includes its history, where it is grown, its medicinal and culinary uses and its principal properties. At the beginning of this directory, you will find an alphabetical index of the spices by their common name.

Black pepper in classic vinaigrette—an essential ingredient.

COOKING WITH SPICES

Here are all the tips any cook will need to prepare and use spices. Also included are recipes for spicy butters, oils, drinks, salad dressings, bouquet garni, chutneys (relishes of fruits, spices and herbs), pickles, curries, puddings and spicy ice cream.

Garam masala is one of the better-known spice combinations.

SPICE COMBINATIONS

We have included some of the more commonly known spice combinations such as curry powder, garam masala and Chinese five-spice, along with some that are less well-known such as alino criolo and sambal.

Chilies come in a variety of shapes and sizes.

THE SWEET PEPPERS

Sweet peppers contain just about the highest concentration of vitamin C you can get. Here you will find some unusual and tasty recipes for preparing and cooking juicy red and green sweet peppers.

THE CHILIES

We all, quite rightly, associate chilies with some of the hottest spices known to cooks the world over. Here you will find information about how to prepare and cook them—and recover afterward.

CUTTING THE MUSTARD

Mustard is one of the oldest and most popular spices. In this section you will learn the differences between some of the best-loved mustards including Dijon, English, American and German.

Spices add extra zest to pickles and relishes.

SPICE VINEGARS

Do you know how to make ginger vinegar or a very spicy vinegar? Now you can learn how to make spicy vinegars quickly and easily to spice up your vinaigrette dressing—and you will find a recipe for Worcestershire sauce.

SPICES FOR BEAUTY, RELAXATION AND HEALTH

Since the very earliest times, ancient people have used spices for cosmetics, soaps, incense, potpourri and perfumes. In this section you will find some unusual and interesting things to do with spices—to make yourself and your home beautiful. While we urge caution against using spices as general medicinal treatments and recommend that you consult a qualified medical doctor, the warming and stimulating properties of some spices are worth knowing about.

THE HISTORY
OF SPICES

Whorld history without the history of spices would be impossible. Spices have been directly responsible for wars, trade routes, the discovery of America, papal edicts and decrees, medicinal cures, cosmetic preparations and religious rituals, not to mention some of the most tasteful cuisine. And they have been traded and used for longer than most people would think.

SPICES AND CHINA

At least 5,000 years ago in China, Emperor Shen Nung was writing a medical treatise extolling the virtues of ginger, cassia, anise and turmeric. He founded spice markets, and his longevity is attributed to the vast amounts of spices he used in his own food. Confucius, around 550 B.C., was advising his disciples not to eat any food that had not been prepared properly with spices.

ARAB TRADERS

At about the same time, the Arab world was trading spices with India. The Indian spice ports on the Malabar Coast were doing a roaring trade in cardamom, ginger, turmeric, peppers, sesame and cumin. Their ships carried pots of growing ginger to ward off scurvy. And the Arabs bought spices from other places—

Spices have been traded for thousands of years.

cinnamon from Sri Lanka; mace, nutmeg and cloves from the East Indies; myrrh from East Africa—as well as produced their own frankincense. The trade routes were long and arduous—traveled by camel caravan from Calcutta or by sea through the Persian Gulf. It was a profitable and lucrative trade, and naturally the Arabs kept the exact location of the spice lands to themselves—and even invented fantastic and ludicrous stories of where the spices came from to throw others off the trail. The Arab traders were the importers and exporters of the spice world. They bought from and sold to places such as Egypt, Persia, Afghanistan and the whole of the Mediterranean—and from there to Europe.

GREECE AND ROME

In ancient Greece and Rome, spices were considered so valuable and important that they were used to flavor just about everything. The Greeks and Romans also wrote extensively about their cosmetic and medicinal applications, but they wasted them too—Nero is said to have burned a year's supply of cinnamon at his wife's funeral (consisting not just of his own personal supply but also the supply for the whole of Rome).

The Greeks liked their food plain and unadorned, and the philosopher Epicurus maintained that although pleasure was what life was all about, it should be simple and enjoyed in moderation. It was he who gave us the word "epicurean." By the time the Greek civilization fell into decline, the Greeks were spicing their food as much as anyone.

THE VISIGOTHS DEMAND PEPPER

As the Roman Empire spread throughout Europe, the Romans took their spices with them and introduced them to the indigenous populations—some of whom already had their own spices. And as the Roman Empire collapsed and the Romans retreated to Rome, they left behind a rich legacy of spices. When the Visigoths blockaded Rome in 408 A.D., one of the ransoms they demanded was 3,000 pounds of pepper.

THE DARK AGES

With the sacking of Rome came 700 years of darkness in Europe. The spice trade continued in the Middle and Far East, but the art of spices was lost in Europe until the crusaders returned from Palestine in the twelfth century with the beginnings of a new trade. Europe woke up again, and the spice trade flourished once more.

THE ITALIAN RENAISSANCE

Venice and Genoa became rich as they capitalized on the new trade, and, from the profits of that trade, the Italian Renaissance was born. Medieval cooking took on a new emphasis and originality—everything had to be spicy and highly colored despite the fact that the spices were so expensive. At one time a horse was valued at the same price as a pound of saffron, while a

sheep could be bartered for a pound of ginger or a cow for two pounds of mace. Pepper was so highly valued that its price was measured in individual peppercorns, and they were used as currency to pay taxes and rent. Later, when peppercorns became less valuable, tenants who were still allowed to pay their rent in peppercorns were considered extremely lucky, and "peppercorn rent" came to mean the exact opposite of what it did originally.

Peppercorns were once used to pay taxes and rent.

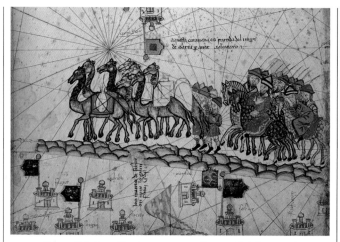

Marco Polo traveling in a caravan (from a Catalan map).

MARCO POLO

But the Arab world still controlled the flow and trade of spices and kept prices high. At the beginning of the thirteenth century, Marco Polo set out from Venice to find a new route to the Far East—one that would bypass the Arab traders. When he returned 25 years later, he brought with him fabulous wealth and treasures from the court of Chinese Emperor Kubla Khan—and spices of course. In fact, nobody back in Venice believed that he had actually made such a fantastic journey until he cooked a magnificent meal for his friends with the new and exotic spices he had brought back with him.

But it would be another two centuries before the Europeans decided that they had had enough of the exorbitant prices and that they really had to do something about it.

❦

HENRY THE NAVIGATOR

Because it was Venice's trading agreements with the Arab world that kept the prices artificially high and provided the Venetians with much of their wealth, it wasn't going to be a Venetian who would seek alternative routes. Enter Prince Henry of Portugal, known as "Henry the Navigator." He financed and equipped expeditions to sail around Africa to find a route into the Indian Ocean. This was in the days of primitive sailing ships that had never before left the sight of land. Prince Henry died without seeing a successful voyage. By 1480 the Portuguese had learned how to sail before the wind, had sailed around Africa and were able to sail to India itself. They reached India in 1497—but not before their great rivals, the Spanish, had become increasingly worried that they might lose out.

CHRISTOPHER COLUMBUS

Vanilla was brought to Europe by Columbus.

The Spanish-employed and unknown Italian Christopher Columbus claimed he could reach India ahead of the Portuguese—not by sailing around Africa, but by sailing westward into the unknown Atlantic. He set sail in 1492 and three months later landed in the West Indies. He was, of course, disappointed. He had set out to find India and instead found America. He returned with allspice from the West Indies, chilies from Mexico and vanilla from Central America.

So almost simultaneously, the two routes opened up, and the spice trade wars really got going. The Spanish and Portuguese found so many ways to interfere with each other's spice trade that the pope was obliged to issue an edict dividing the world into two spice halves—Spain could have everything to the west of an imaginary line in the Atlantic Ocean, while Portugal could have everything to the east.

MAGELLAN

The Spanish employed Magellan (who was Portuguese) to sail westward with five ships and more than 200 sailors to find another route to the Moluccas and the island of Bandaas. They argued that if they approached from the west, they would be within their sphere of influence—and so would not upset the pope, but they would be able to capture the clove and nutmeg market. Magellan did not make it back, but some of his crew and one ship did by rounding the coast of South America.

THE BRITISH AND THE DUTCH

The British and Dutch entered the market in a big way. The Dutch founded the Dutch East India Company to trade directly with India for spices—and the British financed Francis Drake to sail around the world to find another passage to China. War broke out between England and Spain over trade routes. This led to the defeat of the Spanish armada and the British formation of the East India Company.

In 1658 the Dutch fought and beat the Portuguese for the cinnamon trade of Ceylon—and added the pepper ports of Malabar and Java. By 1690 the Dutch had a monopoly on the clove trade—only because they burned all the clove trees growing on any other island except Aboyna. They fiercely kept this monopoly for 60 years until a Frenchman managed to smuggle a ripe fruit off the island and took it to the French colonies, where it was successfully planted.

By the end of the eighteenth century, the British had ousted the Dutch from India, and London briefly became the center of the world's spice trade. But that was not to last for long.

❧

THE AMERICANS

During the American Revolution, the Americans (or colonists, as they were then called) developed swift sailing warships—clippers—to defeat the might of the British navy. After the Americans won the war, these ships sat idle for only a short while before they were put to use sailing to the East Indies—Britain's spice monopoly was broken before it had really begun.

❧

SPICES TODAY

After the ferocious spice trading that went on during the last 600 years, the situation today may seem a little tame. Spices seem to have gradually gone out of favor—no longer do we seek new spice routes or wage war over them. Maybe we have grown used to the less-than-fresh, commercially prepared spices that can be bought in any supermarket. Perhaps it is time to grind a few for ourselves and reawaken our taste buds to the rich aromas and pungent qualities of fresh spices. Or maybe, thanks to the introduction of the refrigerator into virtually every household in

Chilies are native to the Americas.

the Western world, we have so much fresh food that we no longer need spices to mask the taste of less palatable food. Spices, however, are worthy of far more than acting as a cover up—they provide a varied and scintillating range of tastes and experiences.

The current cultivation and distribution of spices is fascinating. Who would have thought that the chilies discovered in Mexico would have been brought to India and incorporated into curries? This has occurred to such an extent that most people today believe that Indian chilies are native to India rather than to the Americas. What is more, who would have thought that Canada would become the world's largest mustard producer?

Spices are no longer regarded as wonders of medicine, but they still play an important part in the manufacture of many cosmetics and perfumes and are grown commercially for their coloring and preservative properties.

Nutmeg and mace are no longer the main crops of the Moluccas, but instead are grown on a large scale on the West Indian island of Grenada.

Cloves, however, still come from Madagascar and Zanzibar—names that are still evocative and romantic and hint strongly of spices.

Nutmeg is grown on a large scale in Grenada.

THE SPICE DIRECTORY

*S*pices have been in use for as long as humans have been cooking their food and as long as herbal medicine has been around, which may be even longer. There is a myth that spices were originally used to disguise the flavor of rancid or less-than-fresh meat, but there seems to be little truth in this. Our taste buds need stimulation and new experiences—and what could better provide this than the spices gathered together for you in the following pages?

We looked at the history of the spice trade earlier, but perhaps a forgotten essential in the use of spices was the invention of the cooking stove. No longer did humans need to cook everything in one pot; they could use several pans—and this meant variety, experimentation and a vast explosion in the use of spices. As the Spanish explorers returned from the New World, they brought not only gold but also new spices—spices never heard of before—and they spread across Europe quickly. There would have been no need for this if spices were used only to flavor meat on its way to going bad—there were already sufficient spices to do that. They spread because people the world over like their food to have a taste, to deliver a surprise, to be interesting and rich.

Now they are the indispensable ingredients in all types of dishes, adding and enhancing existing flavors while at the same time aiding digestion. They complement almost any type of meal, from salads, casseroles and soups to sweet dishes, cakes, pickles and drinks.

The Spice Directory is a comprehensive photographic reference, in alphabetical order by botanical name. It

A pepper mill can be used to grind spices.

covers both common and lesser-known spices, from ginger, cinnamon and pepper, spices that we're all familiar with, to allspice, elecampane and quassia. The directory shows the many different forms in which the spices are available—fresh, dried or ground, in many cases accompanied by a photographic reference of the spice growing as a plant in its native habitat.

Try all or any of the following spices. One or two may need to be used with some caution—especially the chilies. You can experiment and discard any you do not like, but there will not be many of those. These are the best spices the world has to offer. These are spices to improve the dullest cookery; spices to blend and try; spices to find out about and perhaps use for the first time. Most people have the ubiquitous black pepper mill in the kitchen. Now is the time to go out and buy several more—and grind your own spices in them.

We have included the traditional medicinal uses of spices, but you should refer any ailment or condition to a qualified medical doctor before attempting to treat anything yourself at home. We have also included culinary uses, the history of each spice and its origins. There may even be a recipe or two to delight and surprise you.

Have fun and spice it up a bit.

SPICE LIST BY
COMMON NAME

Allspice	*Pimento officinalis*	100
Aniseed (Anise)	*Pimpinella anisum*	102
Asafetida	*Ferula assafoetida*	74
Capers	*Capparis spinosa*	42
Capsicum (Sweet peppers)	*Capsicum annuum*	44
Caraway	*Carum carvi*	54
Cardamom	*Elettaria cardamomum*	70
Cassia	*Cinnamomum cassia*	56
Cayenne pepper	*Capsicum longum*	48
Celery	*Apium graveolens*	36
Chilies	*Capsicum frutescens*	46
Cilantro	*Coriandrum sativum*	60
Cinnamon	*Cinnamomum zeylanicum*	58
Cloves	*Eugenia caryophyllus*	72
Coriander	*Coriandrum sativum*	60
Cubeb	*Piper cubeba*	104
Cumin	*Cuminum cyminum*	64
Curry leaf	*Murrya koenigii*	86
Dill	*Anethum graveolens*	34
Elecampane	*Inula helenium*	82
Fennel	*Foeniculum vulgare*	76
Fenugreek	*Trigonella foenum-graecum*	116
Galangal	*Alpinia officinarum*	32
Ginger	*Zingiber officinale*	122
Grains of paradise	*Aframomum melegueta*	28
Horseradish	*Armoracia rusticana*	38
Java galangal	*Alpinia galanga*	30
Juniper	*Juniperus communis*	84
Lemongrass	*Cymbopogon citratus*	68
Licorice	*Glycyrrhiza glabra*	78

GRAINS OF PARADISE

Aframomum melegueta

*T*he western African tree Amomum melegueta
produces orchidlike, trumpet-shaped flowers in
a beautiful yellow or pink with a yellow
flash, which in turn
produce brilliant scarlet
fruits. It is from
these that we get
the tiny brown
seeds of grains of
paradise, which are
a very unusual,
almost pyramid-
like shape. They are
also known as melegueta
pepper and Guinea grains.

Grains of paradise

Related to cardamom, this spice was once used in place
of pepper when the price of pepper became too high.

ORIGINS & CHARACTERISTICS

Originally from western Africa, grains of paradise are widely
used in both African and Caribbean cooking. The tree grows
only about 8 feet (2½ m) tall and is related to both ginger
and cardamom. Grains of paradise were certainly known
and used in ancient Rome as well as medieval Europe as a
pepper substitute. In Britain they were banned by King
George III (1760–1820), who believed that peppers or any
such hot spices were bad for a person's health.

Culinary Uses

Because the flavor of grains of paradise is hot, spicy and aromatic, they can be used to flavor any dishes in which you would traditionally use black pepper. They can be used in a pepper mill to make an unusual condiment. If you are able to buy the whole seeds from a West Indian or African grocery store, you can then grind them yourself.

Medicinal Uses

In western Africa the seeds are used internally for a wide range of ailments including painful menstruation and excessive lactation. The root of the tree is cooked and used as a treatment for infertility. The best-known use for the seeds is as an aphrodisiac—but you will have to try them out yourself to see if they work.

Recipe
Spicy Jarlsberg Bake
There are several species of grains of paradise. *A. angustifolium* is one of them, and you can cook meat with this pepper. You will need:

- 2 lb (800 g) any meat
- handful of grains of paradise
- 2 cups (500 ml) Jarlsberg cheese
- ⅓ oz (10 g) French mustard
- 1 tsp (2 g) cloves
- ½ cup (125 ml) heavy cream (double cream)

Place the meat in thin slices in a baking tray and sprinkle with ground grains of paradise. Mix the cheese, mustard, cloves and cream and spread over the meat. Bake at 400°F (204°C) for 10 minutes (or until meat is cooked), then grill until golden brown. Serve hot.

JAVA GALANGAL

Alpinia galanga

Galangal originated in China, where it is called Liang-tiang. However, the Java variety, greater galangal is slightly different from lesser galangal (Alpinia officinarum). It is a much bigger plant, growing 10 feet (3 m) tall, with roots more than 3 feet (1 m) long. Java galangal is cultivated in Indonesia and Malaysia, where it is used in cooking to produce a gingerlike flavor in curries and savory meat dishes. In Indonesia it is known as laos and in Thailand as khaa. In Oriental shops it may be sold under any of these names. It is also known as galingale and Siamese ginger.

Greater galangal

ORIGINS & CHARACTERISTICS

The rhizomes (underground stems of the plant) are harvested in the autumn and washed and dried before use. Knobbly and very like those of ginger in appearance, they have a pungent taste and smell like roses. They are lifted, cleaned and then processed in a similar way to both ginger and turmeric. The powdered root is then often mixed with other powdered spices.

Rhizomes

Ground galangal can be added to curries.

CULINARY USES

You can add the powdered root to curries and stews. Because it is subtler than lesser galangal (see page 32), it has a more delicate flavor and is suitable for people who prefer a milder curry. It can be used to flavor sausages. The oil can be extracted and used to flavor soft drinks, liqueurs and bitters. The powdered root can be used in any dish in which you might traditionally use fresh ginger.

MEDICINAL USES

Java galangal is a warming digestive and is used as a remedy for diarrhea, gastric upsets and incontinence. In Asia it is used to treat respiratory problems and congestion, and a drink of grated galangal mixed with lime juice is regarded as a tonic in Southeast Asia. The English variety of galangal, *Cyperus longus*, is used, according to the English physician Nicholas Culpeper (1616–1654), for "expelling wind, strengthening the bowels, helping colic, provoking urine and preventing dropsy." It is also said to be good for fainting spells.

RECIPE
Java Galangal Tea
You will need:
- 1 oz (25 g) powdered root
- 2 cups (500 ml) boiling water

To make Java galangal tea, place the powdered root in a pot and add the water. Steep for half an hour, then strain and let cool. Sip 2 tbsp (30 ml) at a time. This is thought to be a good remedy for liver complaints such as hepatitis and cirrhosis and stomach and digestion upsets.

GALANGAL

Alpinia officinarum

This is the strong Chinese variety of galangal. Its taste and effects are much less subtle, and it is a smaller plant than the Java galangal, growing only to around 5 feet (1½ m) tall. It has been an essential ingredient in Chinese herbal medicine since at least 500 A.D. and is also known as lesser galangal and China root. In China it is called sa leung geung, while its Southeast Asian name is kencur.

Ground galangal

ORIGINS & CHARACTERISTICS

The lesser galangal has spikes of wonderful orchidlike white flowers with red streaks. The roots are washed and dried before they are powdered; they are brown on the outside and orange on the inside. Galangal has been known to the West since the time of the crusades, when the knights brought the root back in the thirteenth century. In Tudor and medieval times, it was used extensively in cooking and as an ingredient in perfume, but it fell out of favor by the eighteenth century. Today it is valued in the West only as a medicine, although in China it is still an important ingredient in soups and stews—it is valued for its warming, gingerlike effect.

CULINARY USES

You can add the powdered root of galingal to any savory dish in which you would use fresh ginger—the taste and effect are very similar. It makes a useful substitute if you cannot get fresh ginger.

MEDICINAL USES

It is taken internally for chronic gastritis, digestive upsets and gastric ulcerations and to relieve the pain of rheumatism. The powdered root can be used to make a poultice to relieve the itch and irritation of skin infections. A tea thought to relieve the pain of gum disorders and mouth ulcers can be made by adding 1 oz (25 g) to 2 cups (500 ml) of hot water and letting it stand for an hour. A tablespoon at a time can be used as a gargle and mouthwash. This tea can be drunk, a tablespoon at a time, to relieve flatulence and indigestion.

RECIPE

Spinach and Galangal Bhaji

You will need:

- 1¾ lb (800 g) cooked spinach
- 1 medium onion
- 4 tbsp (60 ml) butter
- 4 dried red chilies
- 1 tsp (5 ml) cumin seeds
- 2 tsp (10 ml) ground galangal powder
- salt

Chop then fry the onion in the butter and add to the spinach. Then add the chilies, cumin seeds and galangal powder and cook over low heat for 10 minutes. Add salt to taste.

DILL

Anethum graveolens

*T*he name for dill comes from the old Norse word dilla, *which means "to lull"—and dill's mild sedative effect certainly lulls. Dill water, known as gripe water, has been used for centuries to soothe colicky and fretful small babies. It was once, in medieval times, thought to be a magic herb and, as such, was used to combat witchcraft. It was also used in love potions*

Dill seed

for the same reason. Both the seeds and the leaves are used. Dill was not introduced to the United States commercially until the nineteenth century. Nowadays it is mostly grown in the Northern Hemisphere.

ORIGINS & CHARACTERISTICS

Dill is a native of northern Europe and Russia but is now cultivated throughout the world. It is a tall, spindly plant that grows nearly 6½ feet (2 m) tall, with slender stems and fine leaves. The tiny yellow flowers turn into winged seeds at the end of the summer. Both the flowers and seeds are harvested.

Dill weed

Culinary Uses

Dill seeds are strong tasting and warming. They taste similar to caraway, and they can be used to flavor cakes and desserts. You can also use them as a pickling spice for vinegars. The leaves have a less strong flavor and are slightly less bitter. You can add the finely chopped fresh leaves to any fish dishes, salads and sour cream sauces. If you use the leaves in any hot dishes, add them near the end of the cooking time to preserve the flavor.

Medicinal Uses

Dill is rich in sulfur, potassium and sodium and is considered by herbalists to be a completely safe plant. To make gripe water, steep a teaspoon of partly crushed seeds in a glass of hot water for two hours. Strain and add honey for flavor. Make sure it is completely cool before giving it to a baby and give only a teaspoon at a time. Adults are also said to benefit from gripe water if they have upset stomachs because dill is a good aid to digestion; it may also stimulate appetite and help promote milk production in nursing mothers. The seeds can be chewed raw to sweeten the breath and can also act as a digestive aid.

Harvesting & Storage

Pick the fresh leaves at any time to add to your cooking, but to harvest the seeds, pick the flower heads when they are part flower and part seed. Hang the heads upside down in a dry place over a cloth to catch the seeds as they fall. Sow the seeds in a sunny but sheltered garden. Do not plant them near fennel because the two can cross-pollinate.

Dill (Anethum graveolens)

CELERY

Apium graveolens

*F*rom the little wild celery known as smallage that grows wild throughout Europe in river estuaries and salt marshes, we get the cultivated celery from Italy that we have known since the seventeenth century. Smallage, once used as a medicine, would taste very bitter to the modern palate, but the Romans found it useful as a flavoring. They also associated it with bad fortune and death and used the leaves in wreaths. The crisp stems and leaves of cultivated

Celery stalks

celery can be used in salads and cooked with meat stews and casseroles, but the seeds of the wild celery are used as a spice. They are warming and aromatic but quite bitter.

❦

ORIGINS & CHARACTERISTICS

Seeds from the wild celery have been found in the tomb of Tutankhamen, and Culpeper says that the seed "helps the dropsy and jaundice and removes female obstructions" and that the leaves are of the same nature and "eaten in the spring sweeten and purify the blood and help the scurvy."

Celery salt

CULINARY USES

The seeds of the wild celery are quite strong and bitter, so you need very small quantities. They can be used whole to flavor soups and stews or ground and mixed with salt and used as a condiment. To make a warming and spicy tea, grind ½ tsp (2½ ml) of seeds and add to 1 cup (250 ml) of hot water. Allow to stand for 10 minutes and drink it while it's still warm. The juice of cultivated celery stalk can be extracted in a food processor and drunk cool. Celery salt, a salt-based seasoning flavored with the essential oil, is more widely available but soon develops a stale taste.

MEDICINAL USES

A poultice for external use can be made from celery leaves to relieve fungal infections, and the seeds taken internally in small quantities are said to be good for relieving gout, arthritis and inflammation of the urinary tract. Eating the seeds of raw cultivated celery, either by chewing or swallowing them whole, is said to lower blood pressure, to stimulate digestion and to treat rheumatism.

GROWING

To grow your own wild or cultivated celery, plant the seeds in rich, damp soil in a sunny but sheltered position in the spring. The plants do not like frost and will not flower until their second year. Once they have flowered, they will produce seeds readily. The stems of the cultivated celery are best picked and used in the autumn, traditionally after the first frost.

CAUTION

The seeds sold for cultivation should not be used for medicinal purposes because they may well have been treated with fungicides.

Celery (Apium graveolens)

HORSERADISH

Armoracia rusticana

*H*orseradish originated in eastern Europe and is a good kitchen garden plant because its root can be used in a variety of ways to season food. It does need to be contained, however, as it spreads rapidly and, once established, can be a nightmare to eradicate. The root has an extremely powerful flavor. It is used to make the well-known horseradish sauce, in which the combination of ingredients brings out the root's qualities to the best advantage. A homemade sauce is much more flavorful than the commercial variety.

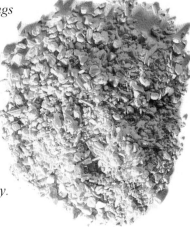

Ground horseradish

ORIGINS & CHARACTERISTICS

Horseradish is a perennial, dark green plant with white flowers. The young leaves can be used for flavoring, but it is the root that most people associate with horseradish. The root has to be dug up fresh because it does not store or keep well.

Horseradish sauce

CULINARY USES

The fresh root has a strong eye-watering pungency (overpowering for some people) and a powerful and stimulating flavor. The fresh root should be grated—carefully to prevent any juice from getting into the eyes—and then added to cream and vinegar to make a sauce that can be used to add zest to fish and, traditionally, roast beef. It makes a good accompaniment to hard-boiled eggs and smoked mackerel. You can make the root a little milder by adding apple to it when you are grating it. You can warm the sauce, but do so very gently because too much heat destroys the oils that give it its pungency.

MEDICINAL USES

Horseradish is a diuretic, which increases urinary flow. It increases perspiration as well, which can be good for some fevers, and it can be made into a poultice to be used

Horseradish (Armoracia rusticana)

externally for wound infections, arthritis and pleurisy. The considerable warming effect of horseradish can cause skin irritation in certain circumstances, and if too much is taken internally, it can cause vomiting and may provoke allergic reactions. Taken internally, it can relieve gout and arthritis as well as urinary and respiratory infections. It should not be given to anyone with stomach ulcers or thyroid problems.

MUSTARD

B. nigra, B. juncea, B. hirta

*T*here are so many varieties of mustard and so much can be made from this one plant that cooks may not need any other kitchen spices. Brassica nigra *is the black mustard, now only grown in peasant economies, which has been replaced in large-scale farming by* B. juncea, *brown mustard. Indian mustard is similar to black mustard—it is also brown and is known as brown mustard. In medieval times mustard was the only spice that the general populace could afford. Mustard has given us some interesting language—"as keen as mustard," "cutting the mustard" and, from the Bible, "The kingdom of heaven is like to a grain of mustard seed."*

Black mustard seeds

Brown mustard seeds

ORIGINS & CHARACTERISTICS

Mustard has been grown for so long that its origins are lost, but it probably came from the eastern Mediterranean, where it grows as a weed and is used for feeding horses. It is a spindly plant that grows around 3 feet (1 m) tall, with bright yellow flowers. The seeds are usually brown or reddish. Real mustard was originally made with fresh grape juice, or the must, from the Latin word *mustum*, hence its name.

Mustard in vinaigrette dressing

CULINARY USES

The young leaves can be cooked as a vegetable, and the flowers can be added to summer salads. The seeds are ground and used as a fiery spice for making mustard, which accompanies many dishes from cold meats to cheeses and is used in sauces for hot dishes. It is also used in vinaigrette dressing. You can use it to add a certain piquancy to sauces for macaroni or baked cauliflower with cheese. Dry mustard powder releases its pungency when it comes into contact with cold liquid. If you use hot liquids, the pungency is reduced or even eliminated altogether—so always make your mustard with cold water. The whole seeds can be used for especially hot curries and for pickling. (See page 158 for additional information—Cutting the Mustard.)

MEDICINAL USES

Traditional mustard plasters were applied as poultices to relieve rheumatism, muscular pain and chilblains. You can soak your feet by wrapping the plaster, soaked in mustard,

*Mustard (*Brassica nigra*) in flower*

around them to ease aches and strains. Mustard plasters may also provide relief for headaches and colds. Remember to use cold water to maximize the heating effect.

CAUTION

People with sensitive skin should take care when using mustard plasters because they can cause blistering. In large doses mustard causes vomiting.

CAPERS

Capparis spinosa

*I*n southern Europe the pickled caper has been used as a condiment for at least the last 2,000 years. The characteristic flavor comes from the capric acid that develops when the flower buds are pickled in vinegar. Capers are used widely in North African cooking as well as in cooking throughout the whole of the Mediterranean—they are especially loved in Sardinia. Increasingly used in the West, they can make a surprising and useful addition to salads or be used as pizza toppings.

Capers

The flower of Capparis spinosa

ORIGINS & CHARACTERISTICS
Capers grow wild through-out the Mediterranean, where they are regarded as weeds. The plant has thick, shiny leaves and short-lived flowers that have purple stamens and fringed white petals streaked with pale pink. It is a beautiful plant and can be grown in temperate climates if it is grown under glass in well-drained soil.

CULINARY USES

The whole pickled caper buds are used in casseroles, stews and lamb dishes as well as in ravigote, tartar and remoulade sauces. They are a good complement to any oily fish and are especially good eaten with salty foods such as salted meat or fish. Capers add an unexpected but refreshing taste to food. They can be added to parsley and sprinkled over beef. They are an essential ingredient in tapenade,

Capers are an essential ingredient in tapenade.

which is an olive paste made in the Mediterranean, and in caponata, which is a Sardinian salad of eggplants and tuna.

MEDICINAL USES

Capers can increase digestion and appetite and induce a general feeling of well-being and vitality. They are thought to be good for gastrointestinal infections and diarrhea. The flower buds can be infused in a tea to ease coughs.

STORAGE

Capers should be kept in a tightly lidded glass jar. Always make sure that they are kept immersed in the vinegar in which they were pickled; otherwise, they will dry out and lose their flavor. It is also best to keep them stored in a dark place.

RECIPE

Caper Sauce

You will need:

- 🌿 1 tbsp each flour and butter
- 🌿 1 cup (250 ml) milk
- 🌿 1 tbsp (15 ml) chopped capers
- 🌿 1 tsp (5 ml) vinegar in which capers were pickled

Melt the butter in a small saucepan and gradually beat in the flour with a wooden spoon. Add the milk little by little, stirring all the time until the sauce is of a medium thick consistency. Then add capers and vinegar.

CAPSICUM (SWEET PEPPERS)

Capsicum annuum

*L*ike chilies, these too are named from the Latin word capsa, *meaning "box," and a pepper is a "box" of seeds. They are milder and more flavorful than chilies and can be eaten raw without any ill effects or burning sensations. They are fresh and juicy with a clear tangy texture and are also known as pimentos.*

Sweet peppers

ORIGINS & CHARACTERISTICS

Sweet peppers are originally from tropical America but are now cultivated the world over in warm climates. They grow on bushes about 3 feet (1 m) tall, with white flowers. The fruits start off green and slowly turn red or yellow as they mature, but the green, immature ones can be used in the same manner as the red or yellow ones.

CULINARY USES

Sweet peppers can be sliced and added raw to salads or used as a salad vegetable on their own. They can be sliced and fried to add to meat sauces. The seeds should be removed before using. The dried and ground flesh of sweet peppers is made into paprika (see page 50). Before cooking sweet peppers, check them for freshness because they go bad easily. Feel for any soft spots and notice any patches of black or brown discoloration. Peppers are excellent pickled or in chutneys and are one of the main ingredients, along with zucchini and eggplant, in French ratatouille (eggplant, zucchini, peppers, tomatoes, etc. cooked in olive oil). The red peppers are sweetest, and the green ones can be quite bitter. You can blanch them for two or three minutes before using to improve the flavor. Peppers can be grilled until they blister and then eaten as a side dish.

Sweet peppers
(Capsicum annuum)

MEDICINAL USES

Sweet peppers contain large amounts of vitamin C, so they are very good for you. They also have revitalizing and antiseptic qualities and are used to stimulate the digestive system.

RECIPE

Andalusian Gazpacho

You will need:

- 4 green peppers
- 4 large tomatoes
- ½ seedless cucumber
- 5 oz (150 g) white bread crumbs
- 1 cup (250 ml) olive oil
- 4 cups (1 l) water
- salt and black pepper
- 2 garlic cloves, crushed
- 1 tsp (5 ml) white wine vinegar

Finely chop the peppers, tomatoes and cucumber. Add to the bread crumbs with a large helping of olive oil. Leave for one hour in water. Put through a food processor or blender. Add salt and pepper to taste. Add the garlic to the vinegar, and pour over the mixture and refrigerate until well chilled. Serve cold.

CHILIES

Capsicum frutescens

*A*lthough related to sweet peppers, there is a considerable difference—mainly the heat. The Latin word capsa *means "box," and a chili is a "box" of seeds. Chilies range in color from red to purple, cream, yellow, green and even black. There is an old saying that the smaller they are, the hotter they are, but be careful—some of the larger ones are really very hot indeed.*

Chilies come in a wide variety of colors.

ORIGINS & CHARACTERISTICS

Chilies were brought to Europe by Spanish explorers returning from South America and are now cultivated throughout the world. There is evidence that they have been grown and used in Central and South America for at least 9,000 years. They can be grown in temperate climates, but they need artificial heat.

Dried, crushed chilies

They grow 6½ feet (2 m) tall, with tiny slender fruits that, when dried, are used as the main ingredient in cayenne pepper and Tabasco sauce. The fresh fruit itself is used in Mexican cooking; generally the seeds are taken out before use. Chilies are best used fresh.

Dried bird's eye chilies

A selection of chili relishes

CULINARY USES

Fresh chilies are used in guacamole, mole poblano and Yucatan soup. They can be grilled until the flesh begins to smoke and blister and then eaten hot—but caution should be used because the fumes can be an irritant. Chilies should be washed under cold water to reduce their fieriness. Indian chilies are used in curries to give them that extra hot quality. Chili powder is cayenne powder (a blend of small, ripe chilies of various origins) mixed with cumin and marjoram or garlic.

MEDICINAL USES

Chilies are used to revive the body, and they are said to help digestion and have a strong stimulant effect. They are warming for colds and chills, and they have good antibacterial properties.

Chili peppers are the fruit of Capsicum frutescens.

CAUTION

Chilies are a very powerful eye and skin irritant—use thin rubber gloves whenever you are handling them fresh. If any of the juice gets on your skin, wash it off immediately with large amounts of cold milk or soap and water. If it should get in your eyes, flush them with generous amounts of cool water. Taken in excess, chilies cause damage to the mucous membranes, as well as digestive and renal problems.

CAYENNE PEPPER

Capsicum longum

*I*f you dry fresh chilies and grind them up,
you have the makings of cayenne pepper—from
which you can make hot sauce and chili powder.
Also known as lal mirch in India and pisihui in
Southeast Asia, cayenne is also
added to ointments for the
treatment of neuralgia,
chilblains and
lumbago. This is
because the
chilies contain
capsaicin, which is
a chemical found
to increase blood
circulation on contact.

Cayenne pepper

As their name suggests, Capsicum longum *are long
and thin and very hot.*

ORIGINS & CHARACTERISTICS

The usual story told about cayenne pepper is that it was
used by the cooks of chuck wagons on the cattle drives
across the Texas plains to flavor some pretty unsavory
meats—such as rattlesnake. A lot of the cooks sowed seeds
of various plants along the cattle trails so that they could
have fresh herbs and spices in later years. This is why there
has been such a spread of spices growing wild in the United
States. Some of these may well have originally not been
native plants.

CULINARY USES

Cayenne pepper is used in hot dishes such as chile con carne. Cayenne can be added to any savory meat dishes in which you want to add heat without necessarily adding extra flavor. You can also add the merest pinch to cheese sauces and spicy mayonnaise (instead of mustard) to give them added color.

MEDICINAL USES

You can infuse cayenne to make a hot, fiery tea thought to stimulate the appetite, relieve stomach and bowel pains and ease cramps. A poultice of cayenne is said to relieve rheumatism and lumbago.

RECIPE
Chile con Carne

You will need:
- 14 oz (400 g) kidney beans
- 1 small onion
- ⅓ oz (10 g) butter
- 1 garlic clove, crushed
- 1¾ lb (750 g) ground beef (minced beef)
- 8 oz (200 g) chopped tomatoes
- 2 tsp (10 ml) cayenne

Whether chile con carne should have beans in it and whether it can include cayenne or only fresh chilies, is debatable, but you can decide which you prefer. Soak the kidney beans overnight and then rinse and boil for 10 minutes; rinse again and boil in salted water until tender, drain and let cool. Chop the onion and fry in the butter and garlic. Add the ground beef and fry together until the beef is browned. Add the tomatoes, kidney beans, cayenne pepper and salt and black pepper to taste. Let simmer for two hours until very thick.

CAUTION
A poultice of cayenne may cause a reaction in people with sensitive skin.

PAPRIKA

Capsicum tetragonum

*P*aprika is made from sweet peppers that have been dried and ground. Ideally only the dried fruit should be used. It has more flavor—lightly pungent and rather sweet—and a lot less heat than cayenne pepper. Instantly recognizable by its bright red color, paprika is the traditional ingredient in Hungarian goulash and in many other dishes from that country. It makes a colorful addition to a wide variety of food including meat,

Paprika

vegetables and barbeque spice mixtures. It is also used as an ingredient in Cajun seasoning.

ORIGINS & CHARACTERISTICS

Although most people consider Hungary as the natural place for paprika to have originated, it was actually introduced there by the Turks. "Paprika" is, however, a Hungarian word, and paprika is the national spice of Hungary, where it is treated with almost religious fervor. It is made only from red sweet peppers, and most paprika outside of Hungary has little in the way of hotness. Its bitterness depends on how much seed is used—ideally only the dried fruit should be used to make good paprika, and the lighter in color the red peppers, the hotter the spice.

Paprika is used to color many dishes.

CULINARY USES

Paprika is used throughout Europe, especially in Portugal
and Spain, but the Hungarians use paprika the most—to
flavor and color many dishes including soups, vegetables,
chicken, fish and meat. But it is mostly known throughout
the world as the key ingredient in Hungarian goulash, a beef
stew. Paprika doesn't keep very well, so it should be bought
in small quantities. You can also use it to garnish canapés
and in sauces for shellfish and shrimp. It also makes an
excellent sauce to serve with lobster or crab.

MEDICINAL USES

It was in 1926 that a Hungarian chemist by the name of
Szent Gyorgi first isolated vitamin C—from paprika. It is
ironic to think of the sailors on the spice routes getting
scurvy, which is caused by a lack of vitamin C, when they
had access to fresh peppers all the time. Paprika has
warming qualities that are thought to make it effective
against cold symptoms, and paprika is a rich and valuable
source of vitamin C and, as such, appears to be the perfect
antidote to winter.

SAFFLOWER

Carthamus tinctorius

*B*ecause it is often called bastard saffron, you
might think that safflower is the poor relation of
saffron, but in reality it is an important spice in its
own right. However, the more unscrupulous traders
will try to sell it as saffron. It has a slightly duller color
than saffron and is more orange—in
fact this is the spice that
produces the bright orange
dye used for Buddhists'
robes—they really ought to
be called safflower robes.
The flowers produce a
yellow dye if they are
processed in water and a red
dye if alcohol is used.
Safflower
Safflower will add color to food but won't flavor it.

❦

ORIGINS & CHARACTERISTICS
Safflower has been cultivated for so long that it is impossible
to say exactly where it originated. It has been found in
Egyptian tombs dating back to at least 3500 B.C. and has
been used in traditional Chinese herbal medicine for a very
long time. The flowers are a bright orange-yellow and are
used for making tea and as a saffron substitute. The oil
processed from the seeds is used as a cooking oil, and the
seeds themselves can be ground and used as a spice.

CULINARY USES

The oil made from safflower is low in cholesterol, so it is very good for anyone on a low-cholesterol diet. You can use the flowers in any recipe in which you would use saffron— they have a slightly more bitter taste but are considerably less expensive.

Safflower tea has many benefits.

MEDICINAL USES

The flower petals can be infused to make a tea that is said to be good as a laxative and to induce perspiration and reduce fevers. Safflower taken as a tea is also good for coronary artery disease and menopausal and menstruation problems, although it should not be given to pregnant women. It may help to reduce the symptoms of jaundice and measles. A poultice made from the flowers is used for reducing skin inflammation and for easing bruises and sprains. Applied externally the flowers are also said to relieve painful and swollen joints.

> **CAUTION**
> Avoid saffron if you
> are pregnant.

STORAGE

The flowers only keep for about a year, so they should be used when they are fairly fresh for the best benefit. They will add a gorgeous color to potpourri, earning their keep despite their lack of aroma.

RECIPE

Safflower Tea
You will need:
- 1 tsp (5 ml) safflower flowers
- 1 cup (250 ml) hot water

For an infusion, steep the flowers in the water. Taken hot, it may induce perspiration. Taken cool, it is said to soothe hysteria.

CARAWAY

Carum carvi

*Y*ou may not think that such a small, nondescript plant could have so many uses or could be so highly prized as a charm against witchcraft and demons. It was also once believed that anything containing caraway could not be stolen, so it was fed to pigeons to stop them from straying. Caraway was also believed to cure venomous serpent bites, prevent hair loss and restore eyesight. It was thought that if a wife placed a few of the seeds in her husband's pockets, he could not have his heart stolen away.

Caraway seed

ORIGINS & CHARACTERISTICS
Caraway grows wild throughout Europe and Asia and has now been naturalized in the United States and Canada. It is cultivated in the Netherlands and Russia on a large scale. It grows only about 8 inches (20 cm) tall, with white or pink flowers.

Caraway (Carum carvi)

CULINARY USES

The leaves can be eaten fresh in salads or added chopped to freshly cooked vegetables. You can add the chopped leaves to cream sauces for a warming, mild flavor not unlike parsley. The leaves and stems can be cooked in stews and soups. If the flowers are picked off early enough, the tap roots will grow larger and can be cooked as a vegetable— they taste like parsnips. The seeds are used to flavor caraway candy, and the oil of the caraway is used to make liqueurs such as kummel. The ground seeds are used in curry powder as well as in flavoring for cakes, breads and biscuits. Caraway is very popular in German and Scandinavian cooking. The gently fried seeds can be eaten with apples or cheese. The seeds are even dipped in sugar and eaten as a confection known as sugar plums.

MEDICINAL USES

The seeds are chewed for immediate relief of indigestion and colic as well as menstrual pains and cramps. The leaves are used to make a tea that may reduce intestinal and uterine spasms as well as relieve gas and indigestion.

RECIPE
Satay Sauce
You will need:
- 1 medium onion, chopped
- 2 cups (200 g) roasted peanuts
- 3 garlic cloves, crushed
- 1 tsp (5 ml) caraway seeds
- 4 tsp (20 ml) coriander seeds
- 3 tsp (15 ml) turmeric
- ½ tsp (2½ ml) cayenne pepper
- 2¾ cups (250 g) coconut flakes
- 2 tbsp (30 ml) soy sauce

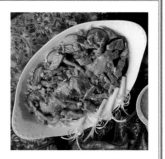

- 1 tsp (5 ml) honey
- 2 cups (½ l) water

Blend everything; simmer until it thickens. Let stand for half an hour before using as a dip or to marinate meat.

CASSIA

Cinnamomum cassia

The bark of cassia, also known as Chinese cinnamon, is a form of cinnamon. Indeed, in the United States, it is used and sold simply as "cinnamon," and in many countries, cassia and cinnamon are used interchangeably. They are closely related, but their taste does differ, cassia being less delicate. It is one of the oldest spices used as a medicine. It was first used in China in 2700 B.C. and in Egypt in 1600 B.C. In Chinese herbal medicine it is known as gui zhi. It is native to Assam and northern Burma.

Cassia bark

❦

ORIGINS & CHARACTERISTICS

Cassia grows in most Asian countries, and the bark is dried in quills for powdering and for using in infusions and tinctures. The twigs and leaves are distilled for their oil—cassia oil contains around 85 percent cinnamaldehyde, which is an important product in the pharmaceutical and food industry. It is also used in the manufacture of cosmetics. The buds are harvested and dried for use as a flavoring in the food industry—they look like cloves.

CULINARY USES

In the United States cassia is used as a sweet spice for flavoring cakes and pastries, while in Asia it is used as a flavoring for curries and savory meat dishes. It is one of the five ingredients in Chinese five-spice (the others being anise, star anise, cloves and fennel seeds). This mixture is used to flavor roasted meats, poultry and marinades. The predominant flavor, however, is star anise.

Chinese five-spice powder

MEDICINAL USES

In Chinese herbal medicine *gui zhi* is used to treat diarrhea, poor appetite, coldness, rheumatism, angina, palpitations and digestive complaints. In the West cassia is a major ingredient in cold remedies, and it is also used to treat dyspepsia, flatulence and colic.

OTHER USES

Making a potpourri mixture

Cassia is sometimes regarded as a poor substitute for cinnamon. However, it has a stronger taste than cinnamon, and some people find that it tastes sweeter and prefer it to flavor mulled wine and sweets. The flowers and dried bark can be used in potpourri. In America cassia is called cinnamon, and in France both barks are known by only one name—*cannelle*. Cassia is much thicker and rougher than true cinnamon and often comes in unrolled lumps, whereas cinnamon usually comes in sticks.

CINNAMON

Cinnamomum zeylanicum

*S*ince ancient times the fragrant, dried inner bark of the cinnamon tree has been a valued spice. The Phoenician traders probably brought it to the Middle East, where it has been used as a perfume since Old Testament times— Moses used it as an ingredient in the anointing oil in the tabernacle. Since the ninth century it has been widely used in Europe, and most of the cinnamon that is used today comes from Sri Lanka.

Cinnamon sticks

ORIGINS & CHARACTERISTICS

In its native habitat this bushy evergreen tree can grow very tall indeed. The deeply veined fragrant leaves are long and dark green with lighter undersides. The flowers are yellow and small and turn into dark purple berries. The bark is the part that is used. Cinnamon can be cultivated from seed or by taking cuttings from a plant. The shoots are cut back every two to three years, and the bark is peeled off and left to dry for a day. The outer bark is stripped away, and the inner bark rolls itself into tight sticks as it dries.

Ground cinnamon

CULINARY USES

For spicing hot drinks such as punch and mulled wine, whole cinnamon sticks are used. They can be used with stewed or fresh fruit and fruit punches. You can use the sticks to stir the flavor of cinnamon into other hot drinks.

MEDICINAL USES

Cinnamon is a strong stimulant for the glandular system and is used to relieve stomach upset. It is very warming, so it is good for relieving the symptoms of colds, flu and sore throats.

Cinnamomum zeylanicum
grows very tall.

STORAGE

Cinnamon is best when bought in sticks, but it can also be bought ground. Ground cinnamon actually tastes stronger, but it should be kept stored in screw-topped glass jars because it loses its smell fairly quickly. The highest quality cinnamon is made from the thinnest bark, which has the best taste and fragrance.

CORIANDER

Coriandrum sativum

*C*ilantro is a small annual herb that grows wild throughout the Mediterranean. The name cilantro is used to refer to the leaves of the plant, and coriander, the spice, refers to the seeds. It was introduced to China around 600 a.d. and called hu, meaning "foreign." It is now cultivated in most parts of the world, including the United States, as an important ingredient in the food industry because it is high in linalol (70 percent), which is used as a flavoring for vegetables,

Cilantro

pickles, seasonings and curries. The name coriander comes from the Greek word koros, meaning "bug" or "insect," because the fruit has an unpleasant fetid smell before it has ripened.

❦

ORIGINS & CHARACTERISTICS
Cilantro grows well in any well-drained soil as long as it is sunny. It grows about 2 feet (70 cm) tall with delicate pink and white flowers. It will bolt if left to dry at the seedling stage. Cilantro grown in warmer climates has much larger fruit than that grown in more moderate regions.

Ground coriander

CULINARY USES

In the Middle East and Asia, especially China, the leaves are used to flavor savory dishes and the seeds are used as a pickling spice. In Thailand the root is cooked with garlic. The whole seeds can be used in cooking fish as well as in breads and cakes. The ground seeds can be added to sausages to give them more flavor, to curries and to roasted meat. In India the seeds are usually lightly toasted before they are ground. The seeds are slightly sweet and have a citruslike taste.

Coriander seed

MEDICINAL USES

Cilantro leaves are used as a remedy for minor digestive problems, and the seeds can reduce the painful stomach spasm effect of some laxatives. Coriander ointment is used externally to relieve the symptoms of hemorrhoids and painful joints. It also stimulates the appetite and is a mild stomach relaxant.

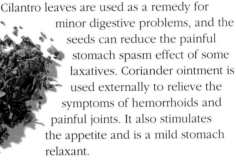

Dried coriander leaf

COSMETIC USES

A good aftershave can be made by infusing coriander seed in alcohol and adding some honey and orange-flower water. If the seeds are harvested in late summer and dried before they are used, the perfume is drawn out. The longer the seeds are kept, the better the scent.

Coriander (Coriandrum sativum)

SAFFRON

Crocus sativus

At times in its history, saffron has been more expensive than gold, and it still is the most expensive spice in the world. It has the same color as well—a deep, dark orange-gold. The slender stigmas of the plant are very light and are handpicked, which accounts for saffron's high value. Luckily very little of the spice is needed to impart its wonderful, slightly bitter taste to cooking.

Saffron

ORIGINS & CHARACTERISTICS

Saffron is made from the dried stigmas of a blue-flowered crocus, which are handpicked in their native Turkey. The plants also grow in surrounding countries, and the very best saffron is said to come from Valencia. A lot of stigmas (around 200–500) are needed to make a tiny amount (1 g) of saffron; that is why it is so expensive.

Purchased saffron comes in two varieties—threads and ground. Ideally you should purchase threads because any artificial dying or coloring is easier to spot in threads. Safflower stigmas are often passed off as saffron, but they are redder in color and don't have the same taste. Turmeric is also sold as saffron, but it is easy to spot because it has quite a different color and taste.

CULINARY USES

Saffron has been used to both flavor and color food since ancient times. It is an essential ingredient in paella, bouillabaisse and risotto Milanese, and, of course, saffron cakes. You can use saffron in a variety of dishes. It flavors shellfish and fish well, and it is a useful ingredient in sauces and rice. Saffron threads should be broken up and infused in a little hot water; the strained liquid should then be added to the dish according to the recipe instructions. You can dry the threads in the oven first and then crumble them into the recipe. The threads should be dark orange with no white streaks. Ground saffron should also be infused before it is used. A mere pinch is enough to flavor rice for four people.

Saffron makes an effective dye.

MEDICINAL USES

You can infuse saffron to make an herbal tea that is taken as a warming, soothing drink to clear the head. It is also believed to shake off drowsiness and bring on menstruation.

OTHER USES

Saffron is also highly effective as a dye. Just a small amount will turn cloth a beautiful light gold color.

CAUTION

Make sure only the stigmas from *Crocus sativus* are used—the unrelated plant, the autumn crocus, *Colchicum autumnale*, is very similar but poisonous.

The flower of Crocus sativus

CUMIN

Cuminum cyminum

*C*umin is a native of the Middle East. It is grown for its seedlike fruit, which is a pungent and aromatic spice slightly similar to caraway. It is mentioned often in the Bible and is a staunch favorite in Greek, Turkish and Arab cooking. The ancient Romans used cumin as a condiment much like we would use black pepper today, but it is probably best known for its role in Indian cuisine— especially curries and chicken roasted in a tandoor (clay oven).

Cumin seed

ORIGINS & CHARACTERISTICS

Cumin will grow in any warm, sunny position in rich, well-drained sandy loam. It grows about 2 feet (60 cm) tall, with very slender stems and tiny pink or white flowers. Indian cumin comes in two varieties—white (*safed*) and black (*kala*). The black cumin has a more subtle flavor but is somewhat expensive and hard to come by outside of India. The fruits are picked before they are fully ripe and left to dry—these are then used ground or whole.

Ground cumin

CULINARY USES

Cumin is used in the spice blend garam masala and is an important ingredient of couscous (cracked wheat steamed and served with meat, vegetables, chickpeas and raisins), which is made throughout the Middle East and North Africa. Cumin is used to flavor meats and cheeses—such as Dutch Edam and the German Muenster. In the Middle East the seeds are often roasted and added to lamb dishes as well as to side dishes of cucumber and yogurt.

MEDICINAL USES

Cumin is taken internally for minor digestive disorders; it is believed to settle stomach upsets that cause migraines. It is a warming appetizer stimulant.

STORAGE

Ground cumin doesn't store well, so it should be bought in small quantities. Whole seeds are difficult to grind with a mortar, so buy both whole seeds and the ground powder.

RECIPE
Spicy Drink with Cumin

A digestive drink is made in India by mixing mint, ginger, salt, sugar, tamarind water and lemon juice with ground cumin. You will need:
- sprig of mint
- pinch of ginger
- pinch of salt
- 1 cup (250 ml) tamarind water
- lemon juice
- sugar
- ground cumin

Mix ginger, cumin and salt into the tamarind water. Add the lemon juice and sugar to taste. Garnish with the mint.

TURMERIC

Curcuma longa

*T*urmeric is a relative of ginger and, like ginger, the spice is obtained from the roots, which are a brilliant orange, and harvested and processed in the same way as ginger. However, turmeric is always traded whole and ground in the consuming country. The roots are boiled, dried, peeled and then ground to produce the bright yellow spice that is used to flavor curries and color mustards, butter, cheeses, drinks and pickles.

Root turmeric

ORIGINS & CHARACTERISTICS

Turmeric grows about 2 feet (50 cm) tall, with large broad leaves and yellow flowers. It is a native of India, but it is now cultivated throughout the world, especially in China, Java, Peru—and India, of course—where some 12,000 tons of it are produced annually. Most of this is exported.

Ground turmeric

CULINARY USES

Turmeric is one of the principal ingredients of curry powder. Although its very strong color is its main attraction, it does have a distinctive taste—like a mild curry flavor, slightly bitter but fragrant. Turmeric is often added to cooking rice to color it a delicate yellow—rice pilaf. Its name comes from the Arabic word *kurkum*, which means "saffron," but the two should not be confused. Saffron is much more expensive and has a different flavor altogether. Turmeric is the flavoring used for Worcestershire sauce as well as the mustard relish piccalilli.

MEDICINAL USES

Taken internally turmeric is thought to be good for

Turmeric is an important ingredient in curry powder.

digestive upsets and skin disorders. It is said to improve poor circulation and ease menstrual problems and is used in Indian herbal medicine for treating liver disorders, uterine tumors and jaundice. It is a strong stimulant of the digestive and respiratory systems and also has anti-inflammatory and antiseptic properties. Externally it can be applied in a poultice to sores and wounds and can be used for ringworm.

Turmeric (Curcuma longa)

STORAGE

Turmeric is almost always sold as a ground powder because the root is very hard to grind. Only small quantities should be bought because it loses its flavor, but not its color, very quickly.

LEMONGRASS

Cymbopogon citratus

*A*lthough lemongrass is a relatively new spice to the West, it should now be available in most supermarkets. Oriental stores sell both fresh and dry lemongrass, sometimes under the Indonesian name "sereh." Its rich lemony flavor and fragrance make it a tangy, spicy addition to many foods. It is a principal ingredient in Thai, Malaysian and Indonesian cooking and curries.

Lemongrass stalks

ORIGINS & CHARACTERISTICS

Lemongrass comes from Southeast Asia and is a tender perennial tropical grass, which can grow nearly 6 feet (2 m) tall. It is densely tufted with long, thin leaves that, when crushed, are extremely fragrant— this is what gives it its name. The flowers are greenish with a red tinge, and they appear in clusters in the summer. You could try growing it yourself—it needs a temperature of at least 55°F (13°C), so that may mean a greenhouse. The leaves, when crushed, add a delightful fragrance to soaps and perfumes.

Ground lemongrass

CULINARY USES

The tender stalks can be chopped, and the leaves, once peeled, can be used in the same way as scallions to flavor stews, casseroles and curries. It should be finely chopped and added just before serving. The base of the leaves is used in sereh, which is a currylike powder used in Southeast Asian cooking, especially with fish and meat. You can make an infusion of the dried leaves to be drunk as an herbal tea. And the finely chopped fresh leaves can be floated on summer drinks.

COSMETIC USES

Lemongrass is used extensively in the manufacture of oils used in making scented soaps because it contains a semidrying property that is excellent for cleansing oily skin.

Lemongrass is used in scented soaps.

STORAGE

The essential oil (citral) loses its effectiveness if it is stored in the light, so it should be kept in a dark cupboard. It will not store for very long, so it should be bought and used fresh.

MEDICINAL USES

Lemongrass is taken internally as a digestive aid for small children and is also used for mild feverish complaints. It is a valuable insecticide and works well externally as a remedy against ringworm, scabies and lice. It is also believed to be an effective treatment for athlete's foot.

Lemongrass
(Cymbopogon citratus)

CARDAMOM

Elettaria cardamomum

There are several varieties of cardamom, each related to ginger and each having a slightly different flavor, but the most common and widely used variety is grown in southern India. Cardamom is both one of the oldest and also highly valued spices in the world—it is the most expensive spice after saffron and vanilla. The Normans

Dried cardamom pods

brought cardamom to Britain in the eleventh century, and it was very popular in medieval and Tudor recipes. Cardamom is mainly used to flavor curries.

ORIGINS & CHARACTERISTICS

The best cardamom comes from the rain forests of Malabar, where it grows as a shrub about 6 feet (2 m) tall, with blue-streaked flowers with yellow tips, and it grows wild throughout India in the tropical mountain forests. It is cultivated in Sri Lanka and Thailand as well as in Central America.

Brown cardamoms

CULINARY USES

In addition to its use in curries, cardamom is used to flavor sausages, breads, cakes and pastries. In the Arab world it is added to coffee as a sign of hospitality because it is one of the most expensive spices—there is also some evidence that it reduces or eliminates the effect of the caffeine in coffee. In northern Europe, especially the Scandinavian countries, it is used mostly as a flavoring for breads and cakes and as a pickling spice, while in Asia it is used as a hot spice for curries, and the whole pods are used as a vegetable. Cardamom is used in India to flavor pilau and curries.

Ground cardamom

STORAGE

Cardamom loses its flavor very quickly, so only very small quantities should be bought. When it is fresh or freshly ground it has a eucalyptus aroma that quickly fades—that is how you can tell if it is fresh. If you buy ground cardamom and it smells of camphor you have been sold a cheap substitute. It is best to buy the whole pods and grind them yourself rather than to buy it already ground (it loses its flavor so quickly when ground that it will already have deteriorated before it can be sold).

The flowers of Cardamom
(Elettaria cardamomum) *are white.*

MEDICINAL USES

Cardamom taken internally may settle upset stomachs and counteract the effects of dairy product allergies. Its warmth is believed to help respiratory disorders, and it is used to revitalize the kidneys.

CLOVES

Eugenia caryophyllus

*T*he name *"clove" comes from the Latin word* clavus, *meaning "nail," which describes its shape. Cloves are the dried flower buds of the clove tree, which is a relative of myrtle. Cloves became known to Europeans by the fourth century as they passed along the spice routes from the East. The Romans and Greeks used cloves extensively in herbal remedies, and there is evidence that cloves were one of the earliest plants used in Chinese herbal medicine.*

Cloves

ORIGINS & CHARACTERISTICS

The clove tree originally came from the Molucca Islands, but cloves are now cultivated in many countries including the West Indies, Zanzibar and Madagascar. The tree is an evergreen with bright red flowers. It grows very tall—more than 50 feet (15 m). The flower buds are dried, and they turn reddish brown. The dried cloves can be used whole or ground, and the taste is extremely strong, pungent and aromatic, so they need to be used sparingly.

Ground cloves

Making orange-and-clove pomanders

OTHER USES

Orange-and-clove pomanders make wonderful aromatic decorations. Pierce the orange with the cloves, pushing them in place in quarter segments of the orange. Dip the orange into a bowl of mixed spices, cover and leave in a dark cool place for a few days, so that they draw in the fragrance.

CULINARY USES

Clove is one of the spices used in garam masala, and it can be used to flavor curries, stocks, sauces, pickles, mulled wine, apple dishes, spiced cakes, mincemeat and marinades for meat and fish dishes. It is a very versatile spice and can be used as an ingredient in sauces as well as to flavor fruit punches. Cloves can be used to give a room a pleasant aroma. Stick several in an orange and hang it up. Cloves also repel insects, so it can be used in your wardrobe instead of mothballs.

STORAGE

Fresh cloves should ooze oil if you press the stalk with a fingernail. Because they are so aromatic, they should be kept tightly sealed in lidded glass jars. And remember that you need very few of them—only half a dozen in an apple pie are enough to flavor it.

Cloves are the dried, unopen buds of Eugenia caryophyllus.

MEDICINAL USES

A whole clove clamped between the teeth is said to relieve toothache. Cloves are also useful for stimulating the digestive system as they are a warming stimulant. They can be taken internally for gastroenteritis and nausea, gastric upsets and impotence.

ASAFETIDA

Ferula assafoetida

*A*safetida is an Asiatic spice that may be known more commonly in the West as devil's dung, or stinking gum. It is hardly surprising, therefore, that it is little known outside India. The name derives from the Persian word aza, *meaning "resin,"* and the Latin word fetida, *meaning "stinking." It is a resin collected from a perennial plant that grows wild in*

Ground asafetida

Afghanistan and eastern Iran. The resin hardens and is sold in lumps, which are ground to a powder and added to vegetables as a delicious flavoring. It also goes well with fish—fresh or salted.

ORIGINS & CHARACTERISTICS

The plant grows around 8 feet (2½ m) tall and is quite foul-smelling, with thick roots. It carries pale yellow-green flowers. The stems are quite thick and are cut to the root, and the milky sap that flows out is collected as a resin, which then hardens. Although it looks like a giant fennel, it is unrelated. In Iran and Afghanistan the leaves and stems are cooked as a vegetable, and the smell, caused by sulfurous compounds, disappears on boiling.

CULINARY USES

Asafetida is mainly used in vegetarian curries, but it can also be used to flavor gravies and stews. The merest pinch added to any fish dish seems to bring out the flavor of the fish and adds an interesting flavor of its own. A little can also be added to relishes.

STORAGE

The ground resin is bright yellow and has a trufflelike flavor when cooked. The ground powder has an unpleasant, strong, garliclike odor and should only be used in minute quantities. Naturally, it should be kept quite separate from other spices in airtight, screw-topped glass jars, or its smell will dominate the aromas of other spices and ingredients.

MEDICINAL USES

Asafetida is believed to clean and restore the digestive tract and relieve stomach pains and colic. It is considered a useful treatment for flatulence, constipation and dysentery. It is said to encourage coughing and, in the East, is given as a remedy for whooping cough and bronchitis. It is sometimes given raw—in pill form to disguise the taste—as an antispasmodic and expectorant.

Ferula assafoetida *in bloom*

FENNEL

Foeniculum vulgare

There are several different types of fennel—from Florence fennel to the sweet fennel—but they are all similar in taste and characteristics, and all of them can be grown in your garden. The leaves of the plant are feathery, making it a decorative addition to the border. The Roman (or vulgar fennel), which tastes like aniseed, has been known for thousands of years as a healing and

The fat bulb root

culinary herb, and the Romans used the shoots as a vegetable, but it is the seeds of the fennel that make an interesting and tasty spice.

❦

ORIGINS & CHARACTERISTICS

Because fennel grows wild in so many temperate places, it's difficult to say where it originated. It was known and used by the ancient Chinese, Romans, Greeks, Britons, Indians, Egyptians and Persians. They all used the young shoots as a

vegetable, dried and ground the seeds as a spice, dried the leaves as a tea and used them fresh as a salad. It was used as an herbal remedy for sore eyes, as a charm against witchcraft and as an antidote for snake bites. The oil was used as a laxative and as a rub for bronchial congestion.

Fennel seed

Baked fennel

CULINARY USES

The leaf bases have a taste like aniseed and can be added to salads. The seeds, dried and bruised, can be used to make a refreshing tea or can be added to fish dishes. The seeds are often sprinkled on the top of bread and cakes. The stems can be dried and chopped and put inside a roasting chicken for flavor. Alternatively, fennel baked on its own is delicious. Fennel seeds are very warming and can be used for adding to any winter stews. You can also finely chop the leaves and add them to yogurt or hummus as an alternative to mint.

MEDICINAL USES

Culpeper says that the leaves or seed "boiled in barley water are good for [nursing mothers] to increase the milk, and make it more wholesome for the child." Fennel is thought to relieve digestive disorders and reduce inflammation. It can be used as a mouthwash and gargle for sore throats.

Fennel (Foeniculum vulgare)

RECIPE

Spicy Herbal Tea

You will need:

- 1 tbsp (15 ml) fresh fennel seeds, crushed
- 1 cup (250 ml) hot water
- honey

Add the seeds to water. Leave to steep for five minutes. Sweeten with a little honey and drink while still hot. For colic and to settle upset stomachs, make a decoction by boiling ½ tsp (2½ ml) of fresh crushed seeds in 1 cup (250 ml) of milk.

LICORICE

Glycyrrhiza glabra

*L*icorice grows widely in the Mediterranean and all the way to China. Its name means "sweet root," and it is cultivated for its flavor and medicinal properties throughout Europe, especially in Italy. It was once used as a cooking sweetener because it has 50 times the sweetening power of ordinary sugar, but since the advent of sugar plantations, it has fallen into disfavor and is now regarded mostly as a weed. This is a shame because it still has a valuable role to play in cooking and medicine.

Licorice sticks

ORIGINS & CHARACTERISTICS

The extremely individual flavor of licorice comes from the root, which is harvested, boiled and filtered and from which the juice is extracted. As it cools, it solidifies into a black, sticky cake. The best of these cakes were always said to be made in Pontefract in northern England, where they still make licorice-flavored candies called Pontefract cakes.

Ground licorice

CULINARY USES

Licorice can be used to add a very strong flavor to beers and liqueurs, or it can be added to pipe tobacco to give it an unusual flavor. Its most common use is as a candy for children. You can buy commercially produced licorice in its sticky black cake form or as a fresh rhizome (the underground stem of the plant). You could always try to grow your own and harvest it yourself.

Licorice (Glycyrrhiza glabra)

MEDICINAL USES

Licorice has a surprising number of uses as a medicinal plant. The dried licorice root or the black extract is used as a vehicle and diluting agent. The root can be chewed or sucked to relieve sore throats and ease other cold symptoms. Licorice is also said to reduce inflammation and spasms, and it is soothing for the lungs because it can expel phlegm and soothe the bronchials If you suffer from indigestion, try licorice; it is also used for treating heartburn and is a gentle, natural laxative. In addition, it may lower blood cholesterol and relieve stomach ulcers. Because of its pleasant, sweet taste, licorice is often added to cough mixtures to mask the bitter taste of some of the other ingredients.

CAUTION

Under some circumstances licorice can lead to a rise in blood pressure, so its use should be kept to a minimum if you have high blood pressure. Avoid licorice if you are pregnant.

STAR ANISE

Illicium verum

*O*ne of the most instantly recognizable spices, star anise is easy to see how star anise gets its name—the shape of the fruit is that of an eight-pointed star. Although unrelated to aniseed, its essential oil is virtually the same, so both plants have the same aroma. Star anise is the fruit of an evergreen tree that originated in the East Indies but

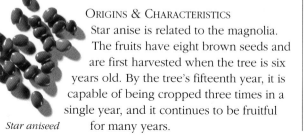

Whole star anise

is now cultivated widely in China, where it is used as a food seasoning and in Chinese herbal medicine. In the West it is often added to fish stews. Its essential oil, which is known as oil of aniseed, is used to flavor liqueurs such as pastis in Italy, Germany and France. Its beautiful shape makes it a welcome addition to potpourris and many decorative projects.

ORIGINS & CHARACTERISTICS
Star anise is related to the magnolia. The fruits have eight brown seeds and are first harvested when the tree is six years old. By the tree's fifteenth year, it is capable of being cropped three times in a single year, and it continues to be fruitful for many years.

Star aniseed

CULINARY USES

The Chinese use star anise in many savory dishes, especially duck and pork recipes, and they often add the ground seeds to coffee and tea to enhance their flavor. The oil is used to flavor drinks. If you need a strong aniseed flavor in cooking, it is even better to use star anise than aniseed.

Star anise enhances coffee and tea.

OTHER USES

The bark can be ground and used as an incense. The Japanese star anise (*Illicium religiosum*) is regarded as a sacred plant, and the tree, which is smaller than star anise, is often planted around temples and near graves. The seeds of star anise can be chewed to sweeten the breath.

MEDICINAL USES

Star anise is a diuretic and appetite stimulant and is also used for relieving flatulence and nausea. In Chinese herbal medicine it is recommended for lumbago, constipation, bladder problems, relieving colic and easing the symptoms of acute rheumatism. It is also used to flavor cough medicines.

STORAGE

Keep the seeds in a screw-topped glass jar to preserve their flavor. You will find the spicy, sweet taste is stronger than anise.

Star anise (Illicium verum)

CAUTION

Do not confuse with Japanese star anise (*Illicium religiosum*). Its fruit is poisonous. But you can tell the difference by the smell— Japanese star anise smells like turpentine.

ELECAMPANE

Inula helenium

*T*his delightfully pretty wild plant grows anywhere in temperate climates that can provide places with the dampness it likes, especially ditches and wet fields, where it can be found in abundance. It is also known as wild sunflower (because of its flowers' similarity to the larger

Elecampane

plant), scabwort and horseheal—the latter two names give some indication of its healing properties when applied externally. It is cultivated widely in the Balkan peninsula.

❧

Elecampane (Inula helenium)

ORIGINS & CHARACTERISTICS
Native to central Asia, elecampane was said to have sprung from the tears of Helen of Troy—hence its Latin name. The rayed yellow flowers look like small sunflowers, and it is a tall, rather attractive plant with oval, downy leaves.

Elecampane is used to flavor vermouth.

CULINARY USES

The flower stems must be removed to encourage root growth, and the roots are harvested after two years, when they are scraped and dried in the sun. They then have a strong, bitter, warm taste. The leaves can be added to salads or used to make a tea that stimulates appetite. The roots can be boiled in water, sliced and used in salads. Elecampane is used to flavor liqueurs such as vermouth. It can be candied to be eaten as a confection. The leaves can be dried and used to make an herbal tea that is said to be good for stimulating the appetite in invalids and sickly children. You can steep the root in wine to make a pleasant cordial drink that is said to cause mirth.

MEDICINAL USES

Elecampane's warming qualities may make it useful as an expectorant to treat bronchitis, asthma and other pulmonary infections. When applied externally as a poultice, the leaves are said to cure scabies, herpes and other skin disorders. It has long been used as a treatment for horse wounds and sores. It is also said to help bring on menstruation and to treat anemia. Soak 3½ tsp (7 g) of the dried root in 4 cups (1 l) of water overnight, then boil for 30 minutes and allow to cool. A small cupful three times a day is said to aid digestion. This mixture can also be used as a gargle and mouthwash. You can also chew the fresh root raw as a breath freshener.

JUNIPER

Juniperus communis

*T*here are many different forms of juniper—from the common juniper to the red cedars of North America. Some such as the common juniper are used medicinally and in cooking, while others such as Juniperus sabina *contain an oil—podophyllotoxin— that is considered too poisonous to use. Juniper has long been considered a magic plant that wards off evil and evil spirits. It was often burned in rooms occupied by the sick, both to fumigate the air and to drive out the demons. Nowadays it is well-known as the spice that flavors gin and other cordials. Juniper berries can be gathered in the wild.*

Juniper berries

ORIGINS & CHARACTERISTICS

Juniper is widespread throughout the world. It grows as a small evergreen shrub or a tree of only about 9 feet (3 m) tall. It carries cones, the females of which turn into berries. The berries start off green and slowly turn black over a three-year period, which is how long they take to ripen.

Juniper is used for flavoring gin.

CULINARY USES

The Latin word *Juniperus* comes from the Dutch word *genever,* which gave us the word "gin." And that is one of the best uses for juniper— flavoring gin. Dried juniper berries are added to patés, game, venison and marinades. They will add flavor to potatoes, sauerkraut, sausages and casseroles. Traditionally they have been used with game because they help to remove some of the stronger "gamey" taste, which some people do not like. Fresh berries are used to make a conserve to accompany cold meats. The leaves can be used fresh or dried with grilled fish, and the wood and leaves can be used on a barbecue to give a subtle flavor to meat.

Juniper (Juniperus communis)

MEDICINAL USES

Juniper is used for urinary tract infections as well as for gout and rheumatism. It can stimulate the uterus and reduce inflammation of the digestive system.

> **CAUTION**
> Avoid juniper if you are pregnant.

RECIPE
Juniper Conserve
You will need:
- juniper berries
- water
- sugar

Cover the berries with water and cook until soft. Crush the pulp and add sugar to the equivalent of three times the weight of the pulp. Beat together vigorously and let cool and set.

CURRY LEAF

Murrya koenigii

*I*n India and Sri Lanka curry leaf is added to curries to strengthen their curry flavor, and it is grown throughout Asia for this purpose; the fresh leaves are widely available. Curry leaves come from a small, ornamental tree that grows wild in the Himalayan foothills. In the West only dried leaves are commercially supplied, and by the time they arrive, they have lost most, if not all, of their flavor. However, there is a Western equivalent, although it is a completely different plant—the curry plant Helichrysum angustifolium. *This is also used as a tea in Africa—Hottentot tea.*

Curry leaves

ORIGINS & CHARACTERISTICS

Curry leaf grows only in tropical regions, so it is not really suited to temperate climates unless it is grown in a greenhouse. Curry plants will grow in any moderate, well-drained soil as long as they get full sun.

Curry leaf is the essential ingredient in Madras curry powder.

CULINARY USES

Curry leaves should be added fresh to curries and spicy meat dishes. The leaves look like bay leaves. They are the essential ingredient in Madras curry powder and give it its unique aroma and flavor. The leaves should be removed before serving. The dried leaves have almost no flavor, but the powdered leaves can sometimes be bought in shops specializing in Indian food. Good storage preserves its flavor. Curry leaves should be added to dishes as a fresh sprig. They are excellent for steamed vegetables to give them a faint curry flavor. They can also be used to flavor rice, soups and stews. The sprig should be removed before it is served. Curry plants give off a very strong aroma of curry.

OTHER USES

Curry plants can be used to give potpourri an aromatic and spicy aroma; the plant has a relative, *H. bracteatum*, which is known as an everlasting flower. Its dry petals will add color to any flower arrangement. It can also be used for garlands and wreaths.

Curry leaf (Murraya koenigii)

MEDICINAL USES

The bark of curry plants is used internally for digestive problems, and the leaves are used as an infusion for constipation and colic. The curry plant has little value as a medicinal plant.

MACE

Myristica fragrans

M *ace is the bright red, shiny fiber that covers the nutmeg seed inside the fruit of the nutmeg tree. It is a weblike form of flesh that, when dried, becomes brittle and turns from red to brownish yellow. Nutmeg and mace, though they both come from the same tree, have different aromas, tastes and uses and should be regarded as two separate spices. Indonesian mace is usually orange-red; mace from Grenada orange-yellow.*

Blades of mace

ORIGINS & CHARACTERISTICS

The fruits of the nutmeg tree are not unlike apricots. The tree is believed to have originated in the Molucca Islands of the East Indies, but it is now cultivated in many countries such as Indonesia, Brazil, Sri Lanka and the West Indies. The Arabs spread the use of mace throughout the Arab world and subsequently all over Europe. During Tudor times in England it was used a lot and considered one of the finest, if not most expensive, spices available. When the Dutch East India Company controlled most of the world's spice trade during the seventeenth and eighteenth centuries, there was a story about how an official in the head office in Amsterdam sent a request to the governor of the Far Eastern colonies to grow fewer nutmegs and more mace because they got more revenue from mace—nutmeg being considered an inferior spice. He didn't realize that they came from the same tree.

CULINARY USES

Nutmeg and mace are used the most extensively by Europeans, both in sweet and savory meals. Unlike nutmeg, which is mainly used as a sweet spice, mace is a strong and aromatic savory spice best suited to baked fish, béchamel sauces, beef stews, casseroles and to season vegetables and potatoes. It should be added just before serving; a little can be grated over the top of any dish.

Ground mace

STORAGE

Mace in its whole form is known as blades of mace and loses its flavor quite quickly; however, it is fairly pungent and should be kept separate from other spices or it will taint them. It should be kept in a tightly lidded glass jar.

MEDICINAL USES

Mace is used to treat stomach disorders such as diarrhea, dysentery and indigestion.

Myristica fragrans *produces both nutmeg and mace.*

NUTMEG

Myristica fragrans

*T*he inner seed of the nutmeg tree, lying inside the filigree covering of mace, is the nutmeg. A nutmeg is quite large—about half an inch (1½ cm) long—and extremely hard. For this reason they are never used whole but is always grated. Once the seed has been separated from the mace, it is left to dry. It can then be grated in very small quantities in hot spicy drinks and used to flavor and sweeten desserts with its warm and highly aromatic taste.

Whole nutmeg

ORIGINS & CHARACTERISTICS

Nutmeg trees grow in hot, tropical places and are extremely difficult to grow. The nutmeg has always been cheaper to produce than mace because it requires little processing before it can be sold, whereas mace has to be dried carefully to prevent decay. The oil of small or damaged nutmeg seeds is extracted and used in the cosmetic industry.

Ground nutmeg

CULINARY USES

You can grate nutmeg over puddings, custards and ice cream, as well as use it to flavor hot spicy drinks such as mulled wine. It is a flavorful addition to stewed fruit such as apples and pears and is used in baking spicy cakes and biscuits.

MEDICINAL USES

In India nutmeg was used as a cure for headaches, insomnia and urinary incontinence. In small doses nutmeg is carminative and is used in treating flatulence and vomiting and for improving overall digestion.

STORAGE

Nutmeg is its own best storage container. Whole spices will keep three or four years. Small quantities can be grated from the whole nutmeg when needed. They should be stored in lidded glass jars.

OTHER USES

Nutmeg is used in the cosmetic industry in soaps, shampoos and perfumes.

CAUTION

Nutmeg contains myristicin, which is a hallucinatory compound and should be regarded as a potential poison. As little as two whole nutmegs could be enough to cause death.

RECIPE

Baked Banana Custard with Nutmeg

You will need:
- 6 ripe bananas
- ⅓ cup light brown sugar (75 g demerara sugar)
- ⅛ oz (5 g) nutmeg, grated
- 1 tbsp (15 ml) lime juice
- 2 cups (500 ml) egg custard
- 2 oz (50 g) bread crumbs

Mash the bananas and mix with the sugar, nutmeg and lime juice. Place in buttered dish. Cover with bread crumbs and add a layer of egg custard. Sprinkle with a little nutmeg and bake at 350°F (176°C) for 35 minutes or until golden brown on top.

MYRTLE

Myrtus communis

*M*yrtle has long been considered a plant of love—it is named after Myrrha, who was a favorite priestess of Venus. Venus transformed Myrrha into the evergreen shrub to protect her from the unwelcome attentions of a suitor. When Paris gave Venus the golden apple for beauty, she was wearing a wreath of myrtle. Myrtle was also planted around her temple. Today it is still woven into bridal wreaths. An Arabic story tells of how Adam gave Eve a sprig of myrtle to declare his love—and she gave him an apple.

ORIGINS & CHARACTERISTICS

Myrtle is an evergreen shrub that grows quite tall—up to 16 feet (5 m)—with glossy leaves that are quite aromatic. The flowers are cream-colored and give way to blue-black berries. In the wild, myrtle grows in dry, hilly conditions in North Africa, southern Europe and the Middle East. The fruits are known as mursins. The flowers can be dried for potpourri, and the leaves and fruit can be used either fresh or dried as an aromatic spicy flavoring for game and roasted meats.

Myrtle (Myrtus communis)

The flowers of myrtle can be dried for potpourri.

CULINARY USES

The branches and leaves, burned on a grill, give meat a delicate, spicy flavor. You can use the fresh leaves to stuff game birds and the dried leaves to flavor stews and casseroles. The fruit, dried and ground, can be added to any savory dishes. The flavor is quite sweet but spicy—not unlike juniper berries.

MEDICINAL USES

Myrtle is a carminative and expectorant and is thought to be helpful in cases of chest infections. The oil is extracted and used to treat acne. In China the dried and powdered leaves were used as an astringent dusting powder for babies when they were wrapped in swaddling clothes. For a tea that may relieve psoriasis and sinusitis, infuse the myrtle leaf—you may need to add honey for taste. A cold compress of the leaves can be used for bruises and hemorrhoids.

NIGELLA

Nigella sativa

*N*igella is known by many other names including nutmeg flower, black cumin, Roman coriander and fennel flower and is a popular spice in Turkey and Tunisia as well as Greece, Egypt and India. The seeds of this pretty, annual herbaceous plant are black and can be dried and ground to provide a fruity-tasting spice. It is related to Nigella damascena, *love-in-a-mist,* with which it is often confused. The two plants are very similar, but only Nigella sativa *should really be used as a spice. The seeds of love-in-a-mist are distilled for an essential oil used in perfumes and lipsticks. They both smell faintly like strawberries. The flowers of Nigella* sativa *are small and white with a blue tinge.*

Nigella seed

ORIGINS & CHARACTERISTICS

Nigella grows wild throughout the whole of Asia and the Middle East, where it has traditionally been used in the same way in which we use black pepper today. In India, where the seeds are called *kalonji,* they are used as a pickling spice. In the Bible they are referred to as "fitches," from the Hebrew word *ketzah,* meaning "vetch." There are 14 varieties of nigella—the most common being love-in-a-mist—and they are mostly grown for their use in dried flower arrangements.

Culinary Uses

You can use the seeds to flavor curries, meat dishes, chutneys, pickles, sauces and cooked vegetables. The Bengalis use them as a flavoring for fish dishes. The seeds can be ground in a pepper mill and used in the same way you would use black pepper. The seeds can be added to breads and pastries to give a little pungency. Because the seeds do have an irritant effect, they should be used sparingly.

Nan bread is flavored with nigella.

Medicinal Uses

Traditionally nigella was given to nursing mothers to increase milk production and to help the uterus recover. The seeds are said to benefit digestion and reduce inflammation or irritation in the stomach lining.

Other Uses

Love-in-a-mist is easy to grow and makes a good flower for dried arrangements (it may take over because it is very invasive). *Nigella sativa* needs more sun and well-drained soil to take well. Sow seeds in the autumn or spring and do not try to transplant. Do not try to grow both as they will cross-pollinate.

The flowers of nigella
(Nigella sativa)

POPPY

Papaver somniferum

*T*he tiny blue-black seeds of the lilac-colored opium poppy, as it is commonly called, were used as a spice by the Sumerians as long ago as 4000 B.C. Nowadays it is cultivated in many countries both for its use as a culinary spice and for its medicinal qualities— it is used to make morphine and codeine.

Poppy seed

ORIGINS & CHARACTERISTICS

Opium poppies grow wild in the Middle East; they were first taken to China a thousand years ago. They have been used

for their pain-relieving properties in ancient Greece, Egypt and Italy, as well as India and the Middle Eastern countries. Opium is obtained from the flesh of the unripe seed heads—the seeds themselves do not contain any of the drug. The plant grows around 4 feet (1¼ m) tall compared with the bright red corn, or field, poppy of Europe. The opium poppy also has a variety with white flowers.

Poppies (Papaver somniferum)

Infusion of poppy seeds

CULINARY USES
In Middle Eastern cooking the seeds are used to flavor sweet dishes and to make cakes, puddings and strudel fillings. In India, which produces an opium poppy with yellow seeds, the seeds are called khas khas and are used to flavor meat dishes. In most European countries the seeds are sprinkled onto newly baked bread to impart a nutty flavor. There is a Jewish three-cornered pastry called hamantaschen, which has a filling completely made of poppy seeds. You can try making cakes of poppy seeds with honey—they were given to the athletes of ancient Greece for extra energy before they took part in the Olympics.

MEDICINAL USES
Opium poppy seeds are used for treating cystitis and pyelitis; make a diffusion and add honey to taste.

CAUTION
In some countries there may be a legal restriction on growing opium poppies; all parts of the plant, except the seeds, are poisonous. The seeds should not be given to anyone suffering from hay fever or any other allergic condition.

RECIPE
Noodles with Poppy Seed
You will need:
- 8 oz (200 g) noodles
- ⅓ oz (10 g) unsalted butter
- 2 tsp (10 ml) poppy seeds
- salt and black pepper

Cook the noodles and add unsalted butter, poppy seeds, salt and pepper to taste. Stir well and eat. This works well as a side dish with a rich meat stew like goulash.

QUASSIA

Picraena excelsa

*T*his spice is also known as Jamaican quassia, or bitter ash. It is similar and closely related to Japanese quassia (Picraena ailanthoides) *and* Surinam quassia (Quassia amara). *They are all deciduous trees from tropical America, India or Malaysia. The word "quassia" describes the bitter compound extracted from the wood and bark; at one time brewers used it instead of hops to flavor beer.*

Quassia chips

ORIGINS & CHARACTERISTICS

The quassia tree grows very tall—over 80 feet (25 m)—and looks a little like the ash tree. It has small, pale-yellow flowers. The wood is used in the form of chips, which are used to flavor tonic wines and beers. If you fill wooden cups made from this tree with water and leave them to stand overnight, you will have a bitter drink that is said to be good for stimulating the flow of gastric juices in the stomach and sharpening the appetite.

CULINARY USES

Quassia chips have an intensely bitter taste but no smell. When added to water or alcohol, they produce a yellow color. Quassia is used in the production of bitters, which were traditionally used in the spring to increase the secretions of digestive juices and stimulate sluggish stomachs, thus restoring the appetite—especially important after a winter of heavily salted and stodgy food.

Quassia amara *tree*

MEDICINAL USES

Only small doses of quassia should be taken for general revitalization. Quassia is also used to treat rheumatism and fevers, stomach disorders and dyspepsia. A tea made from the wood chips is said to be a cure for alcoholism, and an infusion used as a shampoo is said to clear up dandruff. It can also be taken internally as a tea to kill roundworms.

RECIPE
Quassia Tea
You will need:

- 1 oz (30 g) quassia chips
- 2⅔ cups (600 ml) cold water

Steep the chips in water for two hours. Strain and drink. This is said to be equally suitable as a cure for dyspepsia or, poured on the hair, as a cure for lice.

ALLSPICE

Pimento officinalis

*A*llspice is also known as Jamaican pepper and pimento. None of its names is really helpful—it is not a spice combination, and it is not a pepper. Moreover, "pimento" is a word that was used during the Middle Ages to describe any spice. "Allspice" is the name given to this aromatic spice by John

Allspice berries

Ray (1627–1705), an English botanist who thought it tasted like a combination of cinnamon, nutmeg and cloves. It is said to have first been brought back to Europe from its native Jamaica by Christopher Columbus. It was also used by the Aztecs to flavor

Ground allspice

chocolate. Allspice is cultivated in Jamaica on plantations known as pimento walks.

ORIGINS & CHARACTERISTICS

Allspice is the dried fruit of a tree that is native to Central and South America. The flowers are small and white, and the fruits are gathered unripe and dried in the hot sun until they turn a reddish brown. The tree can grow to an enormous height—over 50 feet (15 m).

CULINARY USES

Allspice should be bought whole and ground as needed.
You can use it in much the same way you would use any of
the three flavors it resembles—in hot spicy drinks and
mulled wine; as a pickling spice; for puddings and custards.
It can also be used for meat and fish dishes to which it gives
an unusual and spicy flavor. It's especially good with lamb—
some say it tastes of juniper berries. The leaves are used to
make bay rum, and the flowers can be infused for a tea. You
can add it as a powder to curry dishes and use it to flavor
shellfish. If you can buy the whole berries, you can grind
your own—or try adding a couple to your pepper mill to
add a little zest to your black pepper.

MEDICINAL USES

The oil is distilled and used for flatulent indigestion. It
improves the overall digestion and is said to have a tonic
effect on the nervous system.

COSMETIC USES

You can grate a little into your bath water as an antiseptic
and anesthetic—as well as for its beautiful aroma.

ANISEED (ANISE)

Pimpinella anisum

*T*he oval-shaped, aromatic seeds of
Pimpinella anisum *are one of
the world's oldest known spices. The
ancient Romans were the first to
really discover and use the pungent
and spicy aniseed to flavor their
cakes, which they ate after heavy*

Dutch aniseed

*meals to settle their stomachs. Anise, as it is also
called, is the flavor in the popular Greek drink ouzo.*

Aniseed is used to flavor ouzo.

ORIGINS & CHARACTERISTICS

Aniseed grows wild throughout the Middle East, but it can
also be cultivated in any moderately warm climate. It grows
about 1½ feet (45 cm) tall, with broadish leaves and small
cream-colored flowers that give way to tiny, light-brown
hairy seeds. It was first cultivated by the ancient Egyptians
and then spread throughout the Arab, Roman and Greek
worlds. It has been grown commercially for a very long time
but is now being slowly replaced by *Illicium verum*—star
anise (see page 80) because it is cheaper to grow.

CULINARY USES

The fresh leaves can be used to flavor curries and spicy meat dishes, while the seeds can be chewed to sweeten the breath afterward. The taste is similar to fennel—sweet and spicy—although the leaves have a more delicate flavor. It is used to flavor candy that young children love. And it is also used to flavor various liqueurs such as ouzo, pastis and arak.

The flowers of anise
(Pimpinella anisum)

MEDICINAL USES

Aniseed has warming and stimulating properties and it is these properties that make it useful for treating circulation problems and digestive disorders. It is also soothing for the lungs as an expectorant and is used to both flavor and activate cough medicines. More mysteriously, it is said to avert the evil eye. The oil is used in the production of toothpaste, and aniseed tea is used for settling the digestion and improving overall digestion.

RECIPE

Aniseed Cakes

You will need:
- 3 medium eggs
- ½ cup light brown sugar (100 g demerara sugar)
- 1½ cups (150 g) whole wheat flour
- 2 tsp (10 ml) aniseed powder
- 1 tsp (5 ml) baking powder

Beat the eggs, add the sugar and beat for three more minutes. Mix the dry ingredients together and fold into the beaten eggs and sugar. Drop a spoonful of the mixture into each depression of a cupcake tray and let stand for 12 hours. Bake at 325°F (163°C) for 12 minutes or until the cakes brown nicely. Eat while they are still hot—spread with a little honey for total indulgence.

CUBEB

Piper cubeba

Cubeb is an unusual and very hot spice grown in Sumatra, Penang and New Guinea. It is also known as Java pepper, tailed pepper and tailed cubebs. It is the unripe fruit of a climbing pepper plant that grows like a vine. The dried unripe berries are used, and they look the same as the dried berries of black pepper—both come from the same family and are closely related. Cubeb berries come with little tails attached and, once dried, have a wrinkled, leathery appearance. Compared with pepper, cubeb is a lot more fiery and aromatic. It is used a lot in Indonesian cooking. If the berries are split open, some will have a small seed inside them, while others will be hollow.

Cubeb berries

ORIGINS & CHARACTERISTICS

Cubeb likes rich clay soil with high humidity and lots of shade. It grows well in subtropical forests. The fruits are picked unripe and dried for use in powders, tinctures and liquid extracts or distilled for their oleoresin and oil, which are used by manufacturers to flavor sauces, relishes, bitters and even tobacco. The oil is also used in the production of perfumes and toiletries.

CULINARY USES

Cubeb is used widely in Indonesian food as a hot and spicy pepper addition to rice dishes, curries and fish. It has a taste similar to allspice and can be used to replace this spice when necessary. Be careful—it can be quite bitter if too much is used.

MEDICINAL USES

Because of its warming properties, cubeb is said to relieve coughs and bronchitis, sinusitis and throat infection. Traditionally in Indonesia it was used as an antiseptic against gonorrhea, but there is no evidence of its effectiveness. When the oil is added to tobacco, it is said to relieve hay fever, asthma and pharyngitis. An infusion is made by steeping 1 tsp (5 ml) of powdered cubeb in 1 cup (250 ml) of hot water—a mouthful can be taken three times a day to relieve upset stomachs, indigestion and urinary infections.

RECIPE
Hot Indonesian Rice
You will need:
- 2 onions, finely chopped
- cubeb
- coriander
- cardamom
- turmeric
- 3 cups (250 g) cooked rice, cold
- 3 bananas, as unripe as possible
- 4 eggs

Brown the onions and add the spices—you need to experiment to adjust the quantities to suit your own taste; you could start with ¼ tsp (1¼ ml) of each and adjust accordingly. Add the rice to the onions and spices. Slice the bananas lengthwise and fry. Cook the eggs quite dry— omelet style—and then slice. Serve the rice on a plate with the bananas and sliced eggs around it.

PEPPER

Piper nigrum

*B*lack pepper is not related to sweet peppers. We get peppercorns from the climbing vine Piper nigrum, *which grows in Southeast Asia. The berries are picked unripe and green and left to dry in the sun. Berries that are left to ripen turn red—these are picked and soaked to get rid of the outer dark husk; the inner peppercorn is then dried to become white pepper. The unripe berries pickled in brine are called green pepper, and ripe ones are called pink pepper. Pepper has always been a valuable, expensive spice—we get the term "peppercorn rent" from the way pepper was used to pay taxes and rent during the eighteenth century—and in Roman times it was the most expensive of all spices.*

Black peppercorns

A forest of Piper nigrum

ORIGINS & CHARACTERISTICS
Originally a native of the Malabar coast, pepper is now grown in tropical regions throughout the world; mainly in India, the East Indies and Asia. Black pepper has a strong, pungent flavor, while white pepper has a milder flavor but is sharper, hotter and less aromatic. Peppercorns can be bought whole or ground, but ground pepper does lose its flavor more quickly.

CULINARY USES

Pepper contains a volatile oil that actually helps in the digestion of meat and high-protein foods by stimulating the digestive juices. There are few savory dishes that do not benefit from a little black pepper being added to them after they have been tasted. White pepper is generally used in pale-colored dishes in which the use of black pepper would spoil the appearance. Sauces can be made from the whole peppercorn; they are also used in pickling spices and marinades.

MEDICINAL USES

Pepper is said to be very good for stimulating the digestion, warming the bronchial passageways and relieving congestion.

Clockwise from top: ground black pepper, black and red pepper, tropical mixed peppercorns, coarse ground black pepper, ground white pepper

Piper nigrum *is a perennial vine.*

SUMAC

Rhus coriaria

*T*here are two distinct types of sumac that can be used as spices—the Middle Eastern variety Rhus coriaria, *known as Sicilian sumac, and the North American sumac* Rhus aromatica. *Altogether there are more than 250 species of sumac. Some are quite poisonous, so care needs to be taken to make sure the right ones are used. The Chinese sumac* Rhus chinensis *is used widely in herbal medicine for treating coughs and mouth ulcers but has no culinary use. Sumac is not very well known in the West but can be procured from some Middle Eastern shops in its ground form.*

Ground sumac

ORIGINS & CHARACTERISTICS

Sumac is valued for its high tannin content and its astringent properties. It is related to poison ivy and grows wild as a tall shrub in thickets. The roots are harvested and dried, and the outer bark is stripped off. The fruits are collected when ripe, left to dry and then powdered for use.

Sumac is often used to decorate hummus.

CULINARY USES

In Lebanon the dried fruits are used in the same way in which we use lemon juice in cooking—as a souring agent. The seeds are crushed and then steeped in water to extract the juice. You can also buy sumac powder, which you add to savory dishes to give them a sharpish bite. In Turkey powdered sumac is commonly added to hummus, both to enhance the flavor and to act as a decoration. The North American native peoples used to make a cordial drink from the fresh red berries.

MEDICINAL USES

Sumac is taken internally for treating severe diarrhea, and the root bark is used to treat dysentery. The fruits are used for treating urinary infections. The root bark is also used externally for treating hemorrhoids. A tea made from the bark or leaves is said to be good as a gargle for sore throats. The North American native peoples made a poultice from the fresh red berries to treat the irritation of poison ivy.

OTHER USES

The tree's bark and leaves can be used as a dye.

> **CAUTION**
> Make sure you don't confuse the sumacs—some species are poisonous. Do not use the ornamental sumac.

Sumac (Rhus coriaria) *is a deciduous shrub.*

SESAME

Sesamum indicum

*S*esame is a valuable and important addition to any cook's spice cupboard. It is also one of the earliest spices known to have been used both for its seeds and the oil contained in them. It is recorded in use in Egypt around 5,000 years ago, and there is evidence that it was being cultivated commercially in India as far back as 1600 B.C. Sesame was once

Sesame seed

believed to have magical powers. Ali Baba's famous phrase, "open sesame," probably springs from the seedpods' tendency to burst open suddenly.

❦

ORIGINS & CHARACTERISTICS

Sesame is a native of India, Indonesia, Africa and China; it grows well in sandy soil and needs a hot climate. It is a tall annual with white, trumpet-shaped flowers that turn into seed capsules about 1 in (2½ cm) long. They burst open when ripe and have a sweet, nutty flavor when lightly roasted. Some cultivated varieties do not burst, which makes them easier to harvest.

The Greek sweetmeat halvah is made from ground sesame seed.

CULINARY USES

The ground sesame seed is used as a paste in tahini, which is used in Greek cuisine and is made into halvah, a sweetmeat eaten with strong coffee in the Middle East. Sesame seeds are sprinkled onto bread and cakes. Toasted sesame seeds can be added to vegetables and cheese sauces and used instead of bread crumbs on fish pies. Sesame oil is used widely in cooking. Sesame seeds are also an important alternative to nuts for anyone with a nut allergy. They are used commercially in the production of margarine and cooking oils and even in soaps and lubricants.

MEDICINAL USES

There are few conditions that have not been treated at some time with sesame seeds. This spice can help with hair loss, dysentery, dizziness, headaches, osteoporosis and boils. Because the seeds are very high in calories, they are good for convalescent people. They also make a mild and gentle laxative.

Sesame (Sesamum indicum)

COSMETIC USES

The oil from sesame is used by Mediterranean women for dry skin conditions because it softens and penetrates well. It is also a good suntan oil because it absorbs most of the ultraviolet rays and is resistant to water, so it will not wash off if you go swimming.

WHITE MUSTARD

Sinapsis alba

*T*he seeds of the white mustard are larger and much milder than those of the black mustard and are a pale brown or yellow. They are used in American mustard and mixed with black mustard to make English mustard. They are not used in French mustard. The herbalist Culpeper recommended that white mustard be applied to the soles of the feet in a poultice for *"fevers and*

Yellow mustard seed rheumatic and sciatic pains—to act upon the nerves whenever a strong stimulating medicine is wanted and not excite heat," while Pliny once observed that mustard "has so pungent a flavor that it burns like fire." Pliny also noted 40 remedies that were made using mustard.

ORIGINS & CHARACTERISTICS
White mustard is thought to have originated in the Mediterranean but will grow well in any temperate, dry climate in heavy, sandy soil. It is an annual, growing about 3 feet (1 m) tall, with yellow flowers that turn into seed pods about 1 inch (3 cm) long. The seeds are harvested, dried and ground.

White mustard (Sinapsis alba)

CULINARY USES

White mustard has a pleasant, nutty flavor and is not as hot as black mustard, so it can be used more freely in cooking. The seeds can be used for pickling and can be sprouted with cress to make "mustard and cress"— because the mustard seeds grow more quickly they should be sown three days later. A mustard made with white mustard seeds is quite mild and is traditionally used to accompany American hot dogs and barbecued meat. Use a little grape juice with your mustard powder if you want to reduce its fieriness—use cold water if you want it full strength.

MEDICINAL USES

In Chinese medicine white mustard is used to treat bronchial congestion, colds, coughs and rheumatic joint pains.

CAUTION

Mustard contains substances that can irritate mucous membranes and is also a skin irritant, so home medicinal use should be avoided.

RECIPE
Herb Mustard
You will need:

- 2 oz (60 g) white mustard seed (use powdered if you can't get the seed).
- ¼ tsp (1¼ ml) herb pepper
- 2 oz (60 g) Mignonette pepper
- ⅓ oz (7 g) each of thyme and marjoram
- ¼ tsp (1¼ ml) lemon peel
- 1 pinch dried rosemary
- ¼ tsp (1¼ ml) orange peel
- 1 tsp (5 ml) honey
- 1 tsp (5 ml) wine or herb vinegar
- pinch of turmeric

Grind the mustard as necessary and add all other ingredients. Mix to a paste and use with cold meats—do not store; consume immediately.

TAMARIND

Tamarindus indica

*T*amarind is known as the date of India, because it has been cultivated in India for centuries. It is widely used in Asian cooking. It is also used in Africa, Iraq and the countries bordering the Persian Gulf in southwestern Asia, in chutneys, curries and relishes. In Tudor times it was appreciated in England as a refreshing

Tamarind pods

summer cordial, tamarind water, having probably been introduced to Europe by the Crusaders.

ORIGINS & CHARACTERISTICS

Tamarind grows as a large, dark pod on the tamarind tree, which is a native of tropical eastern Asia. The fruits can be eaten fresh or dried to make a souring agent and used as one would lemon juice. The taste is both sweet and sour, aromatic and spicy. The tamarind tree grows to a height of some 100 feet (30 m) and can reach more than 30 feet (10 m) in girth. It is now cultivated in the West Indies and has become an important spice ingredient in Mexican cooking.

Tamarind seed

CULINARY USES

Tamarind can be purchased as a fibrous, black, sticky pulp known as tamarind paste, which is the husk without the seeds. You extract the flavor by soaking it in hot water to which a little sugar has been added, and then squeezing it. It is a useful flavor to add to curries, meat or fish, and it has a stronger taste than either lemon or lime juice. It is also available in a dried and ground form.

Taramind block

The flower and fruit of tamarind (Tamarindus indica)

MEDICINAL USES

Tamarind makes an excellent laxative—its action is quite gentle. It is also used to treat fevers, asthma, jaundice and dysentery. Women who experience morning sickness in early pregnancy can eat the fruit to relieve the nausea. It is also said to increase appetite and aid digestion.

RECIPE

Tamarind Water

You will need:
- 2½ oz (50–70 g) tamarind paste
- 8 cups (2 l) water
- 3 tbsp (45 ml) sugar
- ½ sliced lemon

Soak the tamarind paste in the water overnight. Strain and add the sugar and lemon. Bring to a boil and simmer for five minutes. Let cool and strain again. This refreshing cordial makes a pleasant cold summer drink. You can add a little fruit or a sprig of mint to serve.

FENUGREEK

Trigonella foenum-graecum

*F*enugreek is also known as bird's foot and greek clover and is grown throughout the world for its medicinal and culinary uses. The seeds have a mild curry flavor and a bitter aftertaste. It is probably best known in the West for its use in the Middle Eastern sweetmeat halva. Because of its ability to restore nitrogen to the soil, fenugreek is used in the East today as cattle fodder. It is also unusual in being a good source of protein.

Fenugreek seed

ORIGINS & CHARACTERISTICS

Fenugreek was probably first grown and recognized as a useful spice in Assyria some time around the seventh century B.C. It spread to India and China and is now used worldwide. In Egypt it is sold as a dried plant called *hilba* as a remedy for painful menstruation. The leaves are picked in summer and used fresh or dried in infusions. The seeds are collected and dried to be powdered or used whole. The Egyptians used it as an ingredient in their embalming fluids. In Yemen it is ground to a paste and added to vegetable dishes.

Ground fenugreek

CULINARY USES

In India the dried leaves of fenugreek, called *methi*, are a valuable addition to curries. The seeds can be left to sprout and used as a salad vegetable. The ground seeds are used in chutneys and relishes— mango chutney often has the whole seeds in it. The seeds can be lightly roasted to reduce the bitter aftertaste. In Ethiopia it is used as a condiment and in baking bread. You can use the seeds in fried foods, stews and pastries.

Dried fenugreek leaves

Fenugreek
(Trigonella foenum-graecum)

COSMETIC USES

For an infusion that can be used for washing the face and hair, infuse the seeds by using 2 tsp (10 ml) of seeds steeped in 1 cup (250 ml) of cold water for six hours. Then boil for one minute and let cool. This infusion is said to improve skin condition and hair quality. You can always mix the seeds with oil for a stimulating massage oil.

MEDICINAL USES

Traditionally fenugreek has been given to men suffering from impotence and to women to bring on childbirth. The seeds can be infused to treat gastric inflammation, colic, insufficient lactation, poor appetite and digestive disorders. In Chinese herbal medicine they are used to treat kidney disorders and edema.

CAUTION

The seeds should not be given to pregnant women because the saponins that the seeds contain are also used in oral contraceptives and could bring on miscarriage by stimulating the uterus.

VANILLA

Vanilla planifolia

The Spanish brought vanilla to the Old World from South America, and it became one of the world's most important flavorings. It is said that Thomas Jefferson introduced it to North America upon his return from France because he missed its taste in ice cream. Now it's one of the most popular flavors.

Vanilla pods

ORIGINS & CHARACTERISTICS

The Aztecs used vanilla to flavor chocolate. Vanilla is the pod of the climbing orchid, which originated on the east coast of South America. The flowers are small and green and are fertilized by hummingbirds. When it is grown outside South America, as in Indonesia, which now produces around 80 percent of the world's vanilla, it has to be pollinated by hand—there are no hummingbirds in Asia. The beans (also called pods) are picked unripe and treated with steam to ferment them. The vanilla crystals, known as frost, grow on the outside of the bean, which, when dried, is long, thin and quite dark. Synthetic vanilla is now widely available, but it does not have the taste of true vanilla.

CULINARY USES

The Aztecs were right—vanilla flavors chocolate superbly. But you can also use it to flavor custards, ice creams, cakes, rice and other puddings, mousses and soufflés. (Use the whole beans in preparing creams to extract the vanilla flavor from the crystals.) The beans should then be removed,

Store vanilla pods in sugar in an airtight container.

carefully dried and stored and reused. Ideally they should be stored in sugar in an airtight container. The flavor will then leak into the sugar, which can also be used as vanilla-flavored sugar. Essence of vanilla is made by crushing the beans and soaking them in alcohol (the kind you choose depends on the flavor you require).

MEDICINAL USES

Vanilla has few medicinal uses apart from aiding digestion and improving appetite.

OTHER USES

A concentrated form of vanilla is used in perfumery.

Vanilla (Vanilla planifolia) *has waxy, fragrant flowers.*

RECIPE

Iced Vanilla Coffee

You will need:

- 🌿 2 cups (500 ml) strong coffee
- 🌿 1½ cups (375 ml) cold milk
- 🌿 ¼ cup (63 ml) sugar
- 🌿 2 vanilla beans (pods)
- 🌿 3 tbsp heavy cream

Mix all the ingredients together and leave in the refrigerator overnight. Remove the beans, add ice and serve.

SZECHUAN PEPPER

Zanthoxylum piperitum

Szechuan pepper is also known as Japanese pepper, anise pepper, fagara, Chinese pepper, and rather charmingly, flower pepper, which comes from its Cantonese name fahjiu. *A warming stimulant, Szechuan pepper can be used as a condiment in much the same way as black pepper, but it is hotter and more aromatic, and so should be used in smaller quantities. In ancient times it was used as a flavoring in foods and wines that were offered to the gods.*

Dried berries

ORIGINS & CHARACTERISTICS

Szechuan pepper grows in the Szechuan region of China. It grows as a large tree but is now mainly cultivated as a shrub. The leaves are picked fresh and used in cooking, and the bark is stripped and dried for infusions and decoctions. The fruits are picked in summer just before they fully ripen and are dried to make the peppercorns. These can be used in a pepper mill or can be purchased already ground. It is very hot, so beware.

CULINARY USES

Chinese cuisine was often considered bland in the West until the discovery of Szechuan cooking, with its fiery pepper sauces and hot curries—all thanks to Szechuan pepper. The leaves can be used to flavor soups and savory dishes—especially meat. They can be boiled with sugar and soy sauce and even covered in batter and fried.

MEDICINAL USES

Szechuan pepper is a stimulant that works on the spleen and stomach. It also has properties that may lower blood pressure. It is diuretic and antibacterial and is used in Chinese herbal medicine as a local anesthetic. It is very warming and, thus, good for relieving the symptoms of colds and flu.

The leaves and fruit of Zanthoxylum piperitum

RECIPE

Szechuan-Battered Shrimp

You will need:

- 4 tbsp (60 ml) self-rising flour
- ½ tsp (2½ ml) Szechuan pepper
- pinch of salt
- 1 piece gingerroot
- 1 egg
- 5 tbsp (75 ml) water
- light oil for frying
- 3¾ cups (500 g) shrimp

Sift flour, pepper and salt and add finely chopped ginger. Add egg and water and beat to a batter. Heat the oil, dip each shrimp in

batter and deep fry for two or three minutes until golden brown. Serve hot, garnished with scallions and a twist of lemon. Alternatively, boil the shrimp and serve garnished with the pepper, salt, ginger, scallions and a twist of lemon.

GINGER

Zingiber officinale

*U*ndoubtedly one of the most well-known and popular spices, ginger was used widely throughout Europe in medieval times to flavor meat dishes until it fell out of favor in the eighteenth century when the spice wars pushed the price up too high. It was first mentioned in Chinese herbal medicine 2,000 years ago and remains a useful and aromatic spice for use in both culinary and medicinal roles. The young rhizomes of the plant are used for fresh ginger, while dried ginger tends to come from older, more pungent rhizomes.

Fresh rhizome

Dried root ginger

ORIGINS & CHARACTERISTICS
Ginger is a perennial native to tropical Asia and is now cultivated in other tropical areas, especially Jamaica. It is the thick, fibrous root of *Zingiber officinale*, which grows around 3 feet (1 m) tall, with long spikes of flowers that are white or yellow with purple streaks.

Ground ginger

CULINARY USES

Fresh ginger is an important part of Chinese cuisine, but it can also be used to add flavor to savory dishes, especially meat. It can be used to flavor sweet dishes and is probably best known in the West as the flavoring in ginger ale. Preserved and crystallized forms are available commercially. Stem ginger is made from the young shoots. Fresh ginger should be peeled before it is cut into thin strips and added to cooking. Dried ginger is the unpeeled root that has been dried—it should be peeled before grating. Ground ginger can be bought commercially, but it loses its flavor quickly; it is best to buy dried and grind it or to buy it fresh if possible.

Chinese ground ginger

MEDICINAL USES

Recent research has shown ginger to be excellent for settling the stomach, and it is now used as a travel sickness remedy. It is also a valuable source of vitamins A and B and is helpful to women suffering from morning sickness during early pregnancy. The fresh root, if chewed, is said to alleviate sore throats as will ginger tea, which is also good for easing colic and flatulence and stimulating the appetite in invalids.

RECIPE
Ginger Tea
You will need:
- ½ tsp (2½ ml) powdered root ginger
- 1 tsp (5 ml) honey
- 1 cup (250 ml) boiling water

Mix the powdered root with honey in the boiling water; let cool before drinking. A little dash of brandy can be added to treat colds and flu.

COOKING
WITH SPICES

Every country uses spices in its cooking in one form or another. And in each country people from different regions will cook the same recipe in different ways, use different spices and quantities—and probably in every village in every region, there will be changes and additions to even the most basic of recipes. Here we will give you some ideas for basic spice recipes, but there are no rules—no exact quantities can be given for all tastes and preferences. Remember, where appropriate, to bottle and refrigerate as soon as possible.

No real cook would ever be without bouquet garni.

SPICY BUTTERS

A n easy way to use spices in cooking is to make spicy butters. These are very easy to make and are useful for spreading on fish or meat before grilling or after as an accompaniment. Or try spreading them on sandwiches to spice them up, and adding a pat of spicy butter to vegetables—it makes all the difference! You cream the butter, preferably unsalted, and add the spices. You can add a little black pepper and salt to taste if you think it needs it. Form the butter into a roll and chill in the refrigerator. Each of the following recipes is for 9 oz (250 g) of butter.

Paprika Butter: Use 3 tsp (15 ml) of paprika. Good for cooking chicken and grilled lamb.

Mustard Butter: You will need 8 tsp (40 ml) of French or German mustard. Use with grilled meats and fish.

Juniper Butter: Crush 20 juniper berries before adding to the creamed butter. Use with grilled meats.

Horseradish Butter: Use 4 oz (100 g) of finely grated horseradish root. Use with grilled fish and meats.

Cumin Butter: Use 3 tsp (15 ml) of ground cumin seed. Use with vegetable dishes and cheese sauces.

You might like to experiment and make your own from the array of spices available. Some of the spices you could try include cayenne pepper, chilies, sweet peppers, cilantro or coriander, mustard seed, poppy seed and sesame seed.

SPICY OILS

Adding spices to oil imparts extra flavor to your cooking.

Oils, like vinegar, will take up the flavor of spices well as long as they have time to mature. You can add spices to virgin olive oil to impart the flavor to your cooking as you use the oil. Use 25 fl oz (750 ml) of olive oil and add six fresh chilies—green or red—10 juniper berries, 10 sprigs of lemongrass, two sprigs of rosemary, two crushed garlic cloves and 10 black peppercorns. Store for one month before using. You can make up several bottles at a time and experiment by adding other spices—you could make a milder oil by substituting sliced sweet peppers for the chilies; or use cilantro, dill, caraway and fennel seeds instead of peppercorns; or you could use bay leaves instead of rosemary and lemongrass. Be sure to store your oils in the refrigerator.

SPICY DRINKS

How cold winter would be without hot, spicy mulled wines to help us through it; somehow the heat seems to really penetrate and do us some good. But we do not have to limit ourselves to mulled wine—there are spicy punches, mulled ales, possets, spiced ciders, toddies, flips and wassails. In fact, any alcoholic drink can be served hot with some spices added to it.

Mulled Wine: Use a full red wine and add to it 3 tbsp (45 ml) of brown sugar, four cloves stuck into a small orange, 1 tsp (5 ml) allspice, 1 tsp (5 ml) grated nutmeg and three sticks of cinnamon. Heat gently—do not boil as this removes the alcohol—for about 10 minutes. Strain and serve with a slice of orange. Traditionally a well-beaten egg was added to the mull just before serving. You could try heating the mixture with a red-hot poker for that genuine touch.

Lambswool: Mix the flesh of four baked apples with (preheated) 4 cups (1 l) of strong dark beer, 2 cups (½ l) of white wine, one cinnamon stick, 1 tsp (5 ml) of nutmeg and 1 tsp (5 ml) of ginger powder. Remove the cinnamon and strain. You will need to squash the mixture through. Heat again and add a little sugar to taste.

Milk Posset: Heat 2 cups (½ l) of milk and add one glass of white wine. Stir in a pinch of ground ginger and a pinch of ground nutmeg, a little sugar and a squeeze of fresh lemon juice. Serve hot.

SALAD DRESSINGS

Spices can be added to your range of salad dressings to add that little extra bite. Spicy salad dressings make a change from the traditional French dressing and can really transform a humble salad into something special. Here are a couple of recipes to try. Both can be quickly prepared and then kept in the refrigerator for further use.

Spicy Chinese Salad Dressing

You will need:

- 🌿 1 garlic clove, crushed
- 🌿 ½ red chili
- 🌿 1 tbsp (15 ml) sesame oil
- 🌿 1 tbsp (15 ml) sunflower oil
- 🌿 1 tbsp (15 ml) cider vinegar
- 🌿 1 tsp (5 ml) soy sauce
- 🌿 1 tsp (5 ml) sherry
- 🌿 1 tsp (5 ml) sesame salt

Make sure that you have removed the membrane and seeds from the chili. Mix all the ingredients together and store in a glass jar in the refrigerator. This salad dressing goes well with bean sprouts, stir-fried vegetables and tofu.

Spicy Cider Dressing

You will need:

- 🌿 6 tbsp (90 ml) cider
- 🌿 juice of 1 lemon
- 🌿 2 tbsp (30 ml) sunflower oil
- 🌿 2 tbsp (30 ml) apple juice
- 🌿 ½ tsp (2½ ml) ground allspice
- 🌿 ½ tsp (2½ ml) nutmeg, grated

Mix all the ingredients together and store in a glass jar in the refrigerator. You may need to alter the quantities of spices to suit your taste. This dressing is sharp and gives salads a tangy lift without using too much oil.

PICKLING VINEGARS

Good cooks also need a pickling vinegar that can be used for a whole range of chutneys and relishes. There are two main types of pickling vinegar—sweet and malt. The sweet is for pickling fruit and the malt for pickling vegetables.

Pickling vinegar can be used for a whole range of chutneys and relishes.

Sweet Pickling Vinegar

You will need:

- 🌿 1 tbsp (15 ml) coriander seeds
- 🌿 1 tbsp (15 ml) whole cloves
- 🌿 5 blades of mace
- 🌿 1 tbsp (15 ml) whole allspice
- 🌿 2 cinnamon sticks
- 🌿 4½ cups (900 g) white sugar
- 🌿 5 cups (1¼ l) white wine vinegar

Put the spices in a muslin bag. Mix the sugar and vinegar. Put the spice bag into the vinegar and leave to steep for six weeks in a sealed glass jar. Strain and use.

Malt Pickling Vinegar

You will need:

- 🌿 1 tsp (5 ml) whole cloves
- 🌿 2¼ tsp (6 g) white peppercorns
- 🌿 2¼ tsp (6 g) mace blades
- 🌿 1 cinnamon stick
- 🌿 2¼ tsp (6 g) fresh gingerroot
- 🌿 2¼ tsp (6 g) whole allspice
- 🌿 5 cups (1¼ l) malt vinegar

Put all the spices in a muslin bag and steep in the vinegar for five to six weeks in a cool place in a tightly sealed glass jar. Shake the jar occasionally. Remove the spices and strain. Use as required.

A traditional bouquet garni

Bouquet Garni

No real cook would ever be without a bouquet garni—that little bag of herbs and spices to flavor a casserole or stew for winter warmth. They are traditionally made in muslin bags, but you might like to try using the outer leaf of a leek— it will not break up during cooking.

You will need:
- 1 bay leaf
- sprig of thyme
- 1 clove
- 6 peppercorns

Place the ingredients in the bag—or leek leaf—and tie with string. Hang inside the pot while cooking, but tie it to the handle so that it can be retrieved prior to serving.

SPICY CHUTNEYS AND RELISHES

Chutneys are relishes of fruit and vegetables. They make a good accompaniment to cold meats, fish, meat pies and curries. They can range from relatively mild to very hot. The word "chutney" comes from the Hindu word *chatni*, which means "strong sweet relish"—and that's exactly what it is.

Sweet Pepper Chutney

You will need:

- 6½ lb (3 kg) large ripe tomatoes
- 1 lb (500 g) onions
- 3 garlic cloves, crushed
- 3 red sweet peppers
- 3 green sweet peppers
- 1 tsp (5 ml) ground mace
- 1 tsp (5 ml) ground black pepper
- 1 tsp (5 ml) paprika
- grated rind and juice of 2 lemons
- grated rind and juice of 1 orange
- 1 tsp (5 ml) ground ginger
- pinch of cayenne pepper
- 2 oz (50 g) salt
- 2 cups (450 ml) white wine vinegar
- 1 cup (250 g) brown sugar

Seed tomatoes after scalding and peeling them—you only want the flesh, not the seeds. Chop the onions and garlic and add to the tomato flesh in a saucepan. Prepare peppers by removing the seeds and membranes. Slice and add to the pan. Add all the other ingredients and heat gently until all the sugar has dissolved. Stir. Bring to a boil and simmer for two hours, stirring occasionally. When the chutney is thick and rich, you can store it in glass jars. Store in a cool place for two months before using—this is a mild chutney that will go well with cold meats and fish.

Spicy Lemon and Lime Relish

You will need:
- 2 cups (500 ml) olive oil
- 5 lemons
- 5 limes
- 2 tbsp (30 ml) black peppercorns
- 1 chopped dried red chili
- 1 tbsp (15 ml) cumin seeds
- 3 tbsp (45 ml) salt
- 4 garlic cloves, crushed
- 1 tbsp (15 ml) white mustard seeds
- 3 bay leaves
- 1 small piece of fresh ginger, grated

In a saucepan, heat the oil thoroughly and let cool. Slice the lemons and limes into quarters. Grind the peppercorns, chili and cumin seeds together and sprinkle over the lemons and limes. Add the rest of the ingredients and stir thoroughly. Let settle for one hour and then pour into a glass jar. Pour over the cooled oil and leave, sealed, in a warm place for one week, shaking every day. Then store in a dark cupboard for one month. The rinds will then have softened and taken on the spices and oil. Serve with hot curries and plain rice.

This relish should keep for up to six months—if you have not eaten it all by then—and goes extremely well with curries.

CURRIES

Most people think of India and China when they hear of curries, and although they do make up a large part of both Indian and Chinese cuisine, there are many other countries that have curry recipes as well such as Mexico, Thailand and the Caribbean countries.

Match your spices to the curry, so use cardamom, cinnamon, cloves and ginger if you want a fresh sweet flavor; turmeric and fenugreek for a slightly more robust sour taste; and cumin and coriander seeds for a fuller, more solid flavor. Only use 1 to 2 tbsp of ground spice blends in a curry for four people—this keeps the taste distinctive and delicate but not overpowering. Fry the spices when you begin cooking because this will develop their flavors, but be careful not to burn them because they will be bitter if you do. For Malaysian curries you should add lemongrass for that distinctive flavor. Thai curries are always part of a selection of dishes in a main meal, and the hotness is usually offset by a sweeter or blander dish; they often include lemongrass, galangal and kaffir lime leaves.

Curry powder (page 87) and garam masala (page 143), are both dry spice blends you can store for up to four months. You might like to make your own curry paste. You can use this immediately to cook any of the tikka curry dishes—these are hot curries using yogurt that were traditionally cooked in a *tandoor* (clay oven).

Garam masala

Curry Paste

You will need:

- 1½ tsp (7½ ml) cumin seeds
- 1 tsp (5 ml) garam masala
- 1 tsp (5 ml) garlic powder
- ½ tsp (7½ ml) paprika
- 1 tsp (5 ml) turmeric
- pinch of salt
- 2 tbsp (30 ml) wine vinegar
- 1½ tsp (7½ ml) coriander seeds
- 1½ tsp (7½ ml) chili powder
- 1 tsp (5 ml) dried mint
- 1 tbsp (15 ml) water
- 2 tbsp (30 ml) olive oil
- squirt of lemon juice

Grind the seeds in your coffee grinder (which you should keep specifically for this purpose if you do not want your coffee to taste too spicy afterward) and add to the other dry ingredients. Stir well, add the water, lemon juice and vinegar and mix into a thin paste. Heat the oil slowly in a heavy frying pan and stir in the paste. Cook gently until all the water has been absorbed (about 10 minutes). You can then use this paste as is, or you can store it in an airtight glass jar—you might like to pour a tiny amount of oil on top of the mixture to keep it really fresh. Once you have this paste it can be used to make a tikka masala—*masala* means "hot," by the way, so you have been warned.

Chicken Tikka Masala

You will need:
- 4 chicken breasts
- 4 tbsp (60 ml) plain yogurt
- 6 tbsp (90 ml) tikka paste
- 2 tbsp (30 ml) olive oil
- 1 clove garlic, crushed
- 1 onion, chopped
- small piece of fresh ginger, grated
- 1 red chili, chopped
- 1 tbsp (15 ml) almonds, ground
- 1 tbsp (15 ml) tomato purée
- 1 cup (250 ml) water
- 3 tbsp (45 ml) melted butter
- ½ cup (125 ml) heavy cream
- dash of lemon juice

To serve:
- 1 tsp (5 ml) cumin seeds
- 4 sprigs of fresh coriander
- 10 fl oz plain yogurt

Skin and cut the chicken into cubes and put in a bowl with the yogurt and half of the tikka paste. Stir well and let marinate for half an hour. Heat the oil in a heavy pan and fry the garlic, onion, ginger and chili for four minutes and then add the other half of the tikka paste and fry for three minutes. Add the almonds, tomato purée and water and simmer for 15 minutes. Brush the chicken with the melted butter and grill for 15 minutes, turning until cooked through.

You can now put the cooked tikka mixture through a blender if you want a smoother masala—or leave more coarsely prepared if you prefer. Add the cream and lemon juice to the pan with the tikka sauce and add the chicken. Simmer for five minutes. This should be served hot with nan bread and a garnish of toasted cumin seeds, fresh coriander seeds and plain yogurt.

And you probably want to know by now how to cook a spicy rice to accompany some of these curries.

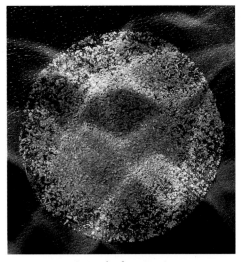

Coriander for spicy rice

Spicy Rice

You will need:

- 🌿 2 onions, finely chopped
- 🌿 ½ cup (125 ml) vegetable oil
- 🌿 1 tsp (5 ml) turmeric
- 🌿 ½ tsp (2½ ml) cumin
- 🌿 ½ tsp (2½ ml) coriander seeds
- 🌿 ½ tsp (2½ ml) cardamom
- 🌿 ¼ tsp (1 ml) cloves, finely ground
- 🌿 1¼ cups (250 g) rice
- 🌿 pinch of salt
- 🌿 2 cups (500 ml) hot water

Brown the onions in the hot oil in a heavy pan, add the spices and fry for two minutes. Add in the rice, washed and drained, and the salt, and brown for two minutes. Add the water so that it just covers the rice (about 1 inch [2½ cm]) and cover and simmer for 15 minutes—or until all the water has been absorbed. Fluff with a fork and serve hot. This is a basic recipe, and you can add any other spices that you want—a little cayenne pepper will give the rice a little bite—or you could swap the turmeric for paprika if you want your rice red rather than yellow. For a plain rice you can leave out the spices and just color it with turmeric or paprika. In India rice is usually fried before boiling, while in China the rice is usually boiled then fried with the meat and vegetables. To make a pilau rice you can add almonds and raisins—lightly sauté them before adding them to the cooked rice.

SWEET AND SPICY TREATS

After you've eaten all that spicy food, what could be better than something a little spicy-sweet to cleanse the palate and sweeten the breath? Spices are not only good for savory dishes but also for candy, puddings and desserts. You may like to try the following recipes.

Cardamom Ice Cream

You will need:

- 16 whole green cardamom pods
- 1 cup (250 ml) whole milk
- 1½ cup (350 ml) heavy cream
- 4 egg yolks
- ⅓ cup (75 g) confectioner's sugar

Bruise 10 of the cardamom pods and heat with the milk and half the cream to almost the boiling point for two minutes. Let cool for 10 minutes. Remove the seeds from the remaining cardamom pods and crush. Whisk the egg yolks with the sugar. Strain the milk mixture and add to the eggs and sugar. Whisk thoroughly and heat until it begins to thicken. Remove from the heat and allow to cool. Whip the other half of the cream and add the crushed cardamom seeds. Fold into the cooled milk and egg mixture. Freeze for two hours. Remove from the freezer and whisk. Return to the freezer overnight or for at least 12 hours.

Spicy Winter Compote

- 1 cup + 2 tbsp (175 g) each of dried peaches, pears, apricots and raisins
- ¾ cup (125 g) confectioner's sugar
- 2⅔ cups (600 ml) water
- ⅔ cup (175 ml) red wine
- 6 allspice berries
- 2 cinnamon sticks
- 6 cloves
- 1 vanilla bean
- 8 peppercorns
- ⅔ cup (175 ml) port

Soak the dried fruit in hot water for 10 minutes. Add the fresh pears, peeled, cored and quartered. Add the sugar and cook over a low heat for five minutes. Add everything else except the port and simmer gently for four minutes. Remove from the heat, add the port and let steep for 10 minutes. Serve warm—it is very good with the cardamom ice cream.

Cardamom Honey Dressing

You will need:
- ½ pint (300 ml) clear honey
- 2 tbsp (30 ml) lemon juice
- a few drops of orange-flower water
- ½ tsp (2½ ml) cracked cardamom seed

Beat honey in a mixer until light in color. Gradually add in the lemon juice and orange-flower water. Stir in cardamom seed. Keep in an airtight jar. This is a delicious dressing for fruit salads.

Vanilla growing up palm

SPICE COMBINATIONS

B y tradition there are various spice combinations that have become known and loved throughout the world. India has produced many spice mixtures for its vast cuisine, possibly the most well known being garam masala, while Europe's famous combination is quatre-épices. There are spice mixtures that are used for specific purposes, such as pickling and pudding spice. However, the following recipes for some of these combinations are the subject of fierce debate and argument. You have been warned. For example, where we might suggest that garam masala is made with only 4 tsp of black cumin seeds, some authorities would argue vociferously that you simply cannot make a good garam masala without using at least five. Or we might suggest that a good curry powder would have, among its other ingredients, 1 tsp of black pepper to 2 tsp of cinnamon, but others will disagree and say that you absolutely, and without exception, must have exactly 2¼ tsp. Combining spices is that sort of area—it allows everyone to find their own particular favorite and become an instant expert. We hope you too will follow this path and become a spice combination connoisseur.

Try to buy seeds and spices that are as fresh as possible. Heat the seeds in the oven for a few minutes or in a heavy frying pan until you can detect the strong aroma. Then you should grind the seeds—a coffee grinder will work for this, but you may find that your coffee tastes a little strange for a while. Or you could have a grinder dedicated specifically for grinding spices. Once ground, the seeds should be put through a coarse strainer to remove any stalks, husks or foreign matter such as small stones. Keep the spices separately in airtight glass jars in a cool dark place and only mix combinations together in quantities that you can use in a week or two at the most; spice combinations will lose their potency quite quickly after that.

All of the following recipes are ones we have tried and like—you may, however, wish to experiment and find your own combinations. All of the recipes are given in teaspoons (ml in parentheses); the quantities refer to flat teaspoonfuls.

It is probably impossible to buy a curry powder in India—people there always mix their own—and you may well be unhappy with the commercially prepared ones—so why not make your own?

Hot Curry Powder

- 2 tsp (10 ml) chili powder
- 1 tsp (5 ml) cloves
- 2 tsp (10 ml) cardamom pods
- 2 tsp (10 ml) ground cinnamon
- 2½ tsp (12½ ml) ground cumin
- ½ tsp (2½ ml) ground fenugreek
- 1 tsp (5 ml) ground nutmeg
- 2 tsp (10 ml) ground black pepper
- 1 tsp (5 ml) mustard seed
- 1 tsp (5 ml) black poppy seed
- 1 tsp (5 ml) curry leaf

Mild Curry Powder

- 1 tsp (5 ml) chili powder
- 1 tsp (5 ml) ground black pepper
- 1 tsp (5 ml) ground cumin
- 4 tsp (20 ml) coriander seeds
- 1½ tsp (5 ml) ground turmeric
- 1 tsp (5 ml) cardamom pods
- 1 tsp (5 ml) ground fenugreek

Mild curry powder. Clockwise from top left: ground fenugreek, ground black pepper, ground turmeric, chili powder, coriander seed, cardamom pods, ground cumin

Garam masala is often mistaken for curry powder, but it is not the same. It might be as hot and as spicy, but it was a different flavor altogether. You can make a dry masala or a wet paste masala. Here are recipes for both.

Garam masala. Clockwise from top left:
ground cinnamon, cloves, ground mace, cardamom pods,
ground cumin, ground black pepper, bay leaves

Dry Garam Masala

- 3 tsp (15 ml) ground black pepper
- 2 tsp (10 ml) ground cinnamon
- 2½ tsp (12½ ml) ground cumin
- 2½ tsp (12½ ml) cloves
- 1½ tsp (7½ ml) ground mace
- 1½ tsp (7½ ml) cardamom pods
- 2 tsp (10 ml) bay leaves

Wet Paste Garam Masala

- 6 tsp (30 ml) coriander seeds
- 3 tsp (15 ml) ground black cumin
- 3 tsp (15 ml) cardamom pods
- 1 tsp (5 ml) bay leaves
- 4 tsp (20 ml) ground black pepper
- 1 tsp (5 ml) ground nutmeg
- 3 tsp (15 ml) ground cinnamon

Add the juice from two lemons (or limes) and make into a paste.

Chinese Five-Spice

Chinese five-spice is used extensively in Chinese cuisine. We have suggested equal quantities for the blend as a starting point—you can then experiment as you will. Be warned, though, that this combination is quite hot.

- ❧ 1 tsp (5 ml) fennel seed
- ❧ 1 tsp (5 ml) aniseed
- ❧ 1 tsp (5 ml) star anise
- ❧ 1 tsp (5 ml) ground cassia
- ❧ 1 tsp (5 ml) cloves

There is a Japanese equivalent, known as seven-flavor spice, which includes pepper leaf, sesame seed, poppy seed, hemp seed, rapeseed and dried tangerine peel. It may be best if you buy this one commercially prepared because getting some of the ingredients may be difficult—if not illegal—in some countries.

Chinese five-spice. Clockwise from top: cloves, ground cassia, star anise, aniseed, fennel seed

French Quatre-Épices
(Four-Spice)

This recipe is a traditional French spice mixture that is used with cold meats and as a general spice blend for seasoning—it is quite hot.

- 🍃 6 tsp (30 ml) ground white pepper
- 🍃 1 tsp (5 ml) whole cloves
- 🍃 1 tsp (5 ml) ground ginger
- 🍃 1 tsp (5 ml) ground nutmeg

French quatre-épices. Clockwise from top left: ground ginger, cloves, ground white pepper, ground nutmeg

OTHER COMBINATIONS

You might like to try your hand at alino criolo, which is a Venezuelan combination of annatto seed, fresh oregano, ground cumin, paprika, garlic salt and black pepper. Fresh garlic is added just before using this in cooking stews and casseroles.

Or how about sambal, which is a spicy relish much loved in India and China? You need fresh chilies, a little sugar, salt, oil, some lemon juice, onion, lemongrass and dried shrimp. They are all blended together to make a hot, spicy picklelike relish to accompany any Indian or Chinese dish.

Others include: Cajun mix, used with Mexican fried beans, which consists of paprika, chili, cumin, mustard and oregano; pumpkin pie mix, which consists of cinnamon, allspice, nutmeg and ginger; and zahtar, used to flavor meatballs and hamburgers—sumac, roasted sesame seeds and thyme.

THE SWEET PEPPERS

Some people have never tried sweet peppers (*capsicum annuum*) because they think they are just fat versions of chilies. Nothing could be further from the truth. Sweet peppers are juicy and tasty without any of the fire that chilies have. Although all chilies are capsicums, not all capsicums are chilies. Sweet peppers are mild and sweet. They can be sliced and eaten raw, added to salads, stir-fried, added to casseroles and stews or stuffed. They can be grilled on their own as vegetables. They are also known as "pimentos" or "bell fruit."

Technically the green sweet peppers are unripe fruit, but they taste very similar to the red and yellow varieties, although they may be a little more bitter. You can blanch them for a minute or two before cooking to remove the bitter flavor. You can also get cream-colored peppers. Before cooking them, you should slit them open and remove the seeds and membrane. These can be quite hot and bitter. If you buy them canned, the seeds should have been removed already, although there should be no need to buy them as such anymore—fresh sweet peppers are now available yearround in most countries.

Sweet peppers should be sliced lengthwise rather than across their flesh as the flavor and juice tend to stay in better.

When buying sweet peppers always look for smooth, firm skins and a good color. There shouldn't be any softness or discoloration. If they have gone soft in any places, they have already started to go bad and should not be bought. Peppers will keep in the refrigerator for three or four days or in a cool pantry for two or three days.

To freeze them, remove the seeds and membranes and slice them lengthwise. Blanch them for two minutes. Cool them under cold running water for two minutes and then drain and freeze them. You can keep them for 12 months in a freezer. When you want to use them, you can add the frozen slices directly to any recipe. If you prefer pepper halves, blanch them for three minutes and defrost for an hour before using.

Sweet peppers are the main ingredient in ratatouille (a French vegetable stew). They make a good accompaniment to grilled meat or baked potatoes.

Ratatouille

You will need:
- 🌿 2 eggplants
- 🌿 salt
- 🌿 5 tomatoes
- 🌿 1 large green sweet pepper
- 🌿 1 large red or orange sweet pepper
- 🌿 6 medium zucchini
- 🌿 3 tbsp (15 ml) olive oil
- 🌿 2 medium onions
- 🌿 2 garlic cloves
- 🌿 ½ tsp (2½ ml) coriander seeds
- 🌿 salt and pepper to taste

Slice the eggplants, sprinkle them with a little salt and let drain. Chop the tomatoes after skinning them. Crush the garlic cloves. Slice open the sweet peppers and remove the seeds and membranes. Slice the zucchini. Peel and coarsely chop the onions.

Heat the oil and gently cook the onions, garlic and peppers for about 10 minutes. Add the eggplant and the remainder of the ingredients. Cover and simmer for about 45 minutes, stirring occasionally to prevent the ratatouille from sticking. You can try experimenting by adding a little Tabasco sauce if you like your ratatouille a little hotter. Garnish your ratatouille with a little finely chopped parsley if you want to add some color.

Grilled Sweet Peppers

You will need:

🌿 selection of sweet peppers

You can use any color of peppers, but remember that the green ones may be a little more bitter than the red or yellow ones. Slice your peppers into two halves and remove the seeds and membranes. Lightly toast on the grill on both sides until the flesh just begins to bubble and brown. You can serve grilled sweet peppers just as they are—hot and succulent. The same technique can be used for adding sweet peppers to kebabs—just cut them into slightly smaller pieces. They slide onto skewers well and should be cooked until the flesh bubbles.

Basque Piperade

You will need:

🌿 1 large red and 1 large green pepper

🌿 6 tomatoes

🌿 2 onions

🌿 1 garlic clove

🌿 4 tbsp (50 g) butter

🌿 6 eggs

🌿 3 tbsp (45 ml) milk

🌿 10 slices of bacon

This is a recipe from the Basque region of Spain.

Prepare the vegetables and garlic in the same way as for ratatouille and cook them all in the butter for eight minutes. Beat the eggs and milk as you would for an omelet. Pour over the vegetables and reduce heat to a simmer. Fry the bacon separately. When the eggs are just set but still creamy on the top, lay the cooked bacon over them and serve hot.

THE CHILIES

No one really knows who grew and used the first chilies—but we do know it was around 9,000 years ago in the Amazon region of South America. Today there are more than 150 varieties of chilies, and they are grown worldwide but principally in Mexico, California, Texas, New Mexico, Arizona, Thailand, India, Africa and Asia.

It was the original inhabitants of Mexico who first discovered chilies and used them in their cooking. Once the Spanish and Portuguese explorers tasted them, their use spread to Europe and beyond. It was not too long before they had made it as far as China. Today chilies are known for their fiery pungency and for enhancing Mexican and Asian cuisine.

Chilies are members of the *capsicum* family (Latin for "box"—a box of seeds). Chilies are the fruit of the *Capsicum frutescens* plant, which will grow in any warm, humid climate, and they are easy to grow at home in pots. They make interesting and useful houseplants. They will cross-pollinate easily, so keep them separate if you want to stick to a particular variety. By tradition the smaller chilies have always been regarded as the hottest, but that may not always be true. Chilies range from mildly hot to the extremely hot, and great care must be exercised when handling them. Ideally you should wear thin surgical rubber gloves and wash your hands afterward. Never rub your eyes or face when handling chilies in any form—the oil they contain is an irritant and will burn. If you do get any on your skin, wash off with very large amounts of cold milk or soap and water. If you get any in your eyes, flush with lots of cool water. If you eat chilies and find them too hot, drink cold milk to reduce the fieriness. Keep chilies away from children.

Chilies come in all shapes, sizes and colors—from long thin ones to short plump ones; from red to green, purple, orange, yellow, cream and black. They can be bought fresh or canned, dried, pickled in brine or powdered. Dried chilies can be hotter than fresh ones, but canned ones are usually milder. If the seeds are used, the chilies will be hotter and more bitter.

PREPARING CHILIES

Fresh chilies should be sliced in half, and their seeds should be removed. You can then lightly grill them, and the skin will peel off easily. They are then ready to use. Some people like to grill them before removing the seeds because there is less risk of the volatile oil getting on their skin. To remove the skin of a chili, drop the chili into a plastic bag and peel it safely in that. Washing chilies will remove the oil—and the pungency. Dried chilies should be lightly roasted and then soaked in hot water for about 10 minutes to rehydrate them. You may need to remove their seeds.

Preparing chilies: once grilled,
the skin should peel off easily.

Remember that the heat of the chilies is in the membrane rather than the seeds, so make sure you remove all of the membrane before use—chilies are hot enough without adding to their fieriness. When buying fresh chilies, look for firm, shiny specimens with good color. They should be dry and heavy. Any that are limp, dull or discolored should be rejected. When you get them home, rinse and dry them and store them in the crisper of your refrigerator. They should keep for two or three weeks. If you do not keep them in the refrigerator, they will deteriorate fairly quickly. They will also spoil if you keep them in a plastic bag because of the moisture build-up. Chilies are hot, but they also have a flavor. Experienced chili eaters will often claim they can experience quite delicate flavors and tastes in chilies that people less used to will not be able to discern. When you first start eating chilies, you will find they all just taste hot, but within a short period of time, you become tolerant to their heat and can both eat hotter varieties and experience their actual flavors. What one person describes as mild or hot may be completely different for another—only you can decide your own preferences. Do not be bullied into eating chilies that are hotter than you really like.

CHILI VARIETIES

Chilies each have a unique flavor and heat level. On the following pages you will find some, but by no means all, of the most popular chilies—each has been graded from one to five for hotness—with five being the hottest.

FRESH CHILIES

Anaheim: This is also known as the Californian chili or the New Mexican chili. It is about 6 in (15 cm) long and either bright green or, fully ripened, red. It looks a little like a sweet pepper (see page 44). When it is dried and powdered, it is sold as "Colorado chili powder." Quite mild—about a one.

Habanero: This is a distinct five+. It comes in any color from red to green to purple and is about 2 inches (5 cm) long. When it is ripe and red, it is said to have a fruity, tropical flavor, but the heat may not let you taste much. This is probably one of the hottest chilies available. It is grown in Central America and the Caribbean.

Anaheim chilies

Jalapeno: This is one of the most commonly used chilies and is grown in Mexico and across the North American Southwest. Dried and smoked, it is known as a chipotle. When fresh, it is a juicy, plump chili about 2 or 3 inches (6–8 cm) long and can be red or, when unripe, green. The red ones are much more flavorsome. A middling heat—a two or three.

Malaguetta: This is a very hot (and tiny) chili from Brazil. Its heat rating is about a five. It is thin and comes in green (unripe) and red (ripe).

Poblano: This one is quite mild—about a two. It is green or red, 4 to 6 inches (10–15 cm) long with quite thick flesh. When it is dried, it is known as an ancho. It comes from Mexico and California.

Scotch Bonnet: Here is another of the very, very hot ones (five+) and is grown in Jamaica and the Caribbean. It is only about 1 inch (2½ cm) long, but it packs a punch. It is usually described as having a smoky, fruity flavor, but the heat may stop you from tasting anything.

Scotch bonnet chilies

Serrano: This is a very thin chili, red or green in color and 2 inches (5 cm) long with quite a clean, sweet taste. It is fairly hot—about a four—but flavorful as well. The red ones are definitely sweeter than the green.

Bird's Eye: This is a tiny chili, but what it lacks in size it makes up for in strength! Very hot—five.

DRIED CHILIES

Chilies are dried because they last longer this way and are easier to transport. Here is a selection.

Ancho: This is the dried poblano chili. It has a sweet, fruity flavor and is quite mild—about a two. It is usually reddish brown with wrinkled skin.

Cayenne: This one is grown and dried in Louisiana and Mexico and is quite hot—about four or five. It is used to make the famous cayenne pepper. It is also what comes to mind when one thinks of chilies—about 2 to 4 inches (5–10 cm) long, bright red and tapering to a point.

Guajillo: A mild dried chili from central Mexico, it is widely available, 4 to 6 inches (10–15 cm) long with a rough, burgundy-colored skin and a slight bitter flavor. The skin is a bit tough and should be removed before using the chili.

Mulato: This is another popular mild dried chili, also from central Mexico, 4 to 5½ inches (10–14 cm) long with a dark brown skin. It has a smoky flavor reminiscent of licorice and rates a one or two for heat.

New Mexican: These come in many colors—from pale olive to bright scarlet. They are quite mild, a one or two, with a full chili flavor not masked by excessive fieriness.

Pasilla: This is a moderately mild chili, about a three, from central Mexico. It is about 6 inches (15 cm) long with an almost black skin, shiny and wrinkled. Some pasillas can be very hot, so choose carefully. You can also get powdered pasilla.

Bird's eye chilies

Using Chilies

Most people will have heard of chile con carne, but there are many other uses for chilies—where would India be without chilies for its curries? The Szechuan region of China produces some very hot chilies for use in Chinese cooking, but it is probably Mexican and Caribbean cuisine that most people associate with chilies—and rightly so. No true Mexican would go very long without eating mole poblano, which is the traditional dish of Mexico—and how about guacamole made with chilies and avocados? In tropical regions, chilies, with their fiery taste, are used to flavor bland tasting staple foods, and in India they are used in rice, as well as a staple ingredient in many curry powders. Chilies are now even used to flavor vodka. As stated before, always remember to exercise caution when using chilies, hold well away from your face when cutting them and don't rub your eyes. If possible, wear a pair of household rubber gloves. Fresh chilies help in digesting starches and are rich in vitamin C. But remember—a little goes a long way.

Mole Poblano

You will need:

- 4 large chicken pieces
- 1 onion, chopped
- 1 tbsp olive oil
- 1 each of pasilla, ancho and mulato chilies (or any 3 dried chilies if you cannot get these), chopped
- 2 cloves garlic, crushed
- 6 tomatoes, chopped
- 2 tbsp (10 ml) sesame seeds
- 2 tbsp (30 ml) whole almonds
- 2 tbsp (30 ml) peanuts
- ½ tsp (2½ ml) coriander seeds
- 1 square dark chocolate

Cook the chicken with the onions and olive oil in a large, heavy pan until the chicken is browned. Remove the chicken and let dry. Add the chilies, garlic and tomatoes to the oil and cooked onions and cook thoroughly for about 10 minutes. Grind all the nuts and seeds, add to the cooking chilies and cook for an additional five minutes. Take a little of the cooked juices, dissolve the chocolate in it and pour into the pan. Put the chicken back in and bring to a boil. Then simmer until the chicken is cooked through. You can add a little water if necessary. Serve hot with a fresh salad.

CUTTING THE MUSTARD

Mustard, being incredibly easy to grow and thriving in temperate climates, is not surprisingly one of the most common and widely used of all the spices. The Romans were probably first to recognize its importance in cooking, and they spread it to all the parts of their empire. As their empire collapsed and they retreated to Rome, they left behind many legacies—one being the use of mustard.

The name comes from two Latin words—*mustum* and *ardere*. *Mustum* means the "must"—the fresh grape juice from newly fermented wine, and *ardere* means simply "to burn"—and that is how mustard was made, with grape juice and at a burning hot temperature. But mustard should always be made with cold liquid—grape juice, vinegar, water; if it is made with hot liquid, the pungency and heat is eliminated. If that is what you prefer, that is fine, but to preserve the fiery nature of mustard, cold liquid must be used.

There are two basic types of mustard—brown and white. The brown mustard seeds are more aromatic and tasty, while the white ones are larger and hotter. Mustards the world over are combinations of these two types of seeds.

English mustard is made from a combination of both white and brown seeds (roughly 20 percent white and 80 percent brown) mixed with flour and turmeric. It is often sold as a dry, bright yellow powder. Cold water is added to this to make a traditional

English mustard is often sold as a dry, bright yellow powder.

hot English mustard. It should always be allowed to stand for 10 minutes to let the flavor develop.

French mustards are of two types: Dijon and Bordeaux. Dijon is made from brown seeds that are husked and ground and mixed with verjuice (unripe grape juice). Dijon mustard is used to flavor mayonnaise and sauces.

Bordeaux mustard is made with whole seeds and mixed with vinegar, sugar and tarragon. It is used as an accompaniment to cold meats.

German mustards are very similar to Bordeaux mustards, but they are usually flavored with spices, herbs and caramel, which tend to make them darker and tastier. They are good with cold meats and sausages.

American mustard is made from powdered white seeds and flour, vinegar and coloring. It is excellent with hot dogs and hamburgers.

French Dijon mustard

MUSTARD COMBINATIONS

English Whole-Grain: This is a pungent, hot mustard made from whole white seeds with white wine, black pepper and allspice.

Green Peppercorn Mustard: It is made with Dijon mustard with crushed green peppercorns added to it and is popular in Burgundy, where it is eaten with grilled meat. It is quite hot and spicy.

White Wine Mustard: This is another Dijon mustard made with white wine. Quite hot, it is used for flavoring sauces.

English whole-grain mustard

Tarragon Mustard: This Bordeaux-type mustard is flavored with tarragon. It is quite mild and is excellent with other spicy foods.

Düsseldorf Mustard: As its name implies, it is very popular in Düsseldorf. Although a type of German mustard, it is without the spices and caramel, but it is not nearly as mild as German mustard and is best eaten with spicy food.

Moutarde de Meaux: This is a Dijon mustard made with whole brown seeds—nicely hot and best eaten with foods that are not so spicy.

Coarse Grain Mustard: This is a type of Moutarde de Meaux which has white wine added to it. It is quite hot.

Florida Mustard: This is a Bordeaux mustard made with wine from the Champagne region rather than vinegar.

Once you have tried all of the commercially available mustards, you can try experimenting with your own. Try mixing white and brown seeds, husked or whole, adding herbs and spices, using vinegar or wine—even adding a little honey, caramel or garlic.

Mustard can be used in a vast variety of ways in cooking, adding extra zest to pickles, relishes and salad dressings. It would be a shame not to build on this still further by exploring all the different mustards you can make and adding even more flavor. Mustard makes a wonderful addition to all cheese dishes, really bringing out the flavor of the cheese. Cheese on toast will never taste the same again! And mustard mayonnaise spices up ordinary salad dishes.

Mustard Mayonnaise

You will need:

- 1 egg yolk
- ½ tbsp (2½ ml) mustard of your choice
- ½ tsp (2½ ml) Worcestershire sauce
- 1 tsp (5 ml) white wine
- salt and pepper to taste
- 3 drops Tabasco sauce
- 1 cup (250 ml) fine cooking oil such as sunflower or olive oil
- the juice of ½ lemon

Blend together everything except the lemon juice in a little of the oil. Add the rest of the oil—blending slowly. Then add lemon juice while still blending. This mayonnaise is excellent for salads.

SPICE VINEGARS

It is hard to believe that the vinegar we use to make vinaigrette dressing and to pickle and preserve spices and herbs is actually an acid—and so corrosive that you should only use stainless steel, earthenware, glass or enameled pots when using it in cooking.

Vinegar is made from the fermentation of wine, cider or malted barley and flavored with herbs or spices.

The best wine vinegar is made by slowly fermenting wine until it turns acetic. It should then stand for a month before use. You can get red wine vinegar and white wine vinegar. Both are fairly strong, so you should use wine of the same color to dilute them. Most people use white wine vinegar in vinaigrette dressing and mayonnaise because red wine vinegar will turn everything pink—red wine vinegar is, however, the most flavorful.

Malt vinegar is made from malted barley and is brown in color. This color is added by mixing the vinegar with caramel. Malt

From left to right: cider vinegar, red wine vinegar, malt vinegar, sherry vinegar.

vinegar used to be judged by its color—the darker the brown, the stronger the vinegar, but nowadays it is often colored artificially. Malt vinegar is best used for pickling.

Cider vinegar is, as its name suggests, made from fermented cider. It has a distinctive taste and is halfway between wine vinegar and malt vinegar in strength. Cider vinegar is best used for chutneys and fruity relishes.

You can also get sherry vinegar—made from sherry and used by French chefs to make poulet au vinaigre—as well as distilled vinegar and spirit vinegar. Distilled vinegar is colorless and used for pickling white onions. Spirit vinegar is very strong and flavored with lemon juice—it is slightly alcoholic.

To make the following spice vinegars, you can use any of the vinegars mentioned here, but a good white wine vinegar may be best, although a distilled vinegar will give you a purer flavor of the spices.

Basic Spice Vinegar

You will need:

🌾 spice seeds—approximately 2–3 tbsp (30–45 ml) spice to 4 cups (1 l) vinegar

Lightly bruise any spice seeds in a mortar. Put the crushed seeds into the vinegar and shake well. Put the spice vinegar in a warm, dark place for two weeks and give it an occasional shake. At the end of this time, taste the vinegar. If you want a stronger tasting spice vinegar, strain off the mixture and discard the seeds. Use the vinegar with a fresh batch of spices and ferment again. Taste again at the end of two weeks. You can do this as many times as you want until you reach the required strength. Once will be enough with most spice vinegars. When you have the desired strength, strain off the seeds and store your new vinegar in a corked bottle. These vinegars can be used to make mayonnaise and vinaigrette sauces or poured over salads. They can also be used as pickling vinegars.

TYPES OF SPICE VINEGARS

Mustard Vinegar: Use 3 tbsp (45 ml) of crushed mustard seeds to 2 cups (750 ml) of vinegar (all recipes employ the same amount

of vinegar). You can use white or brown or try a combination of both.

Chili Vinegar: Use six hot red chilies and one whole garlic clove. Leave for two weeks and make sure you strain thoroughly. You can try experimenting with different types and different strength chilies.

Coriander Vinegar: Use 3 tbsp (45 ml) of crushed coriander seeds.

Ginger Vinegar: Use one whole root peeled and finely chopped.

Spicy Vinegar: Use 1 tbsp (15 ml) of crushed black peppercorns, 1 tsp (5 ml) of crushed celery seed, 1 tsp (5 ml) of peeled and chopped fresh gingerroot, one dried chili, one cinnamon stick, 1 tsp (5 ml) of allspice. Simmer all of the spices together in the vinegar. Let cool and store for two weeks. Strain and bottle.

Very Spicy Vinegar: You need two garlic cloves, six fresh hot red chilies, 2 tsp (10 ml) of black peppercorns, 2 tsp (10 ml) of juniper berries, four sprigs of lemongrass, four sprigs of rosemary. Put all of the ingredients into the vinegar and store for two weeks.

Quick Chili Vinegar: Add 2 tsp (10 ml) of hot chili sauce to the vinegar and use it immediately. Alter the amount of chili sauce to increase or decrease the fieriness.

Worcestershire Sauce: Although not strictly a vinegar, this can be used in the same way. You need six garlic cloves, 1 tsp (5 ml) of black pepper, ¼ tsp (1¼ ml) of chili powder, 1½ cups (350 ml) of vinegar, 5 tbsp (75 ml) of soy sauce. Blend all of the ingredients together in a blender. This is now ready to use, but store it in an airtight bottle and shake well before use each time.

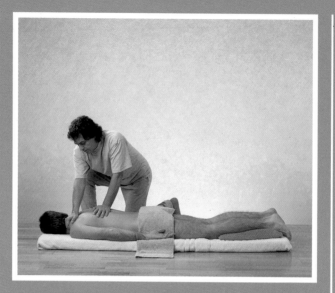

SPICES FOR BEAUTY, RELAXATION AND HEALTH

SPICES FOR BEAUTY AND RELAXATION

Traditionally in the West herbs have had a place in beauty treatments, while spices have been overlooked or considered too hot or pungent to have much use. However, some spices do have beneficial cosmetic uses, and we have included the following for your consideration. Bear in mind that certain skin types are more sensitive than others, so test each of the following potions and recipes before you use them.

In the Orient spices have been associated with beauty, perfume and color for thousands of years. The pungent aroma of spices was used to hide the smells of unwashed bodies and to purify and cleanse the air. Spices have also played a very important part in the manufacture of incense and are coloring agents in dyes for fabrics, carpets and silks.

In the hot climate of Eastern countries, spices were important for adding to oils to soothe and protect the skin from the harsh

Try making your own spicy blends of massage oils.

sun and to add to unguents to keep hair healthy and clean. Spices have been used both as cosmetics and as charms against evil and witchcraft since the earliest times. While nowadays it is easy to go out and buy whatever beauty products we need, nothing quite compares to making our own—an experience that enables us to partake again of a natural world in which the resources of nature are at our disposal.

It may be easier to buy synthetically produced perfumes, face creams, incense and massage oils, but it is not as satisfying as producing your own special and unique blends. Using spices in our beauty treatments creates an air of decadence, wealth, luxury and indulgence that may well be missing in commercial products. Perhaps we are not inclined to go as far as Emperor Heliogabalus, who bathed in hot baths of saffron and not only acquired a delicate aroma but also a healthy-looking golden glow, but we may well want to spice up our bathroom cabinet or add a certain something to the aroma in our homes. Spices are evocative and pungent—they bring the enigmatic Orient, or the sun of the Caribbean, or a hint of the mysterious lost civilizations of South America into our homes. They give us color and grandeur, fragrance and heat.

Using spice in incense goes back centuries.

INCENSE

Most people have at one time or another used incense to add a
spicy aroma to their homes and maybe wondered where and
how this tradition started. Perhaps the earliest cave dwellers
discovered that a handful of certain leaves sprinkled on the dying
embers of a cooking fire would produce a sweet smell that
would mask the smells of leftover food, or maybe they used the
spices in their cooking and when some fell into the heat of the
fire, they liked the pleasant aroma. We will never know, but we
do know that the ancient Egyptians and Babylonians used
incense as part of their religious rites and that incense was used
in China since the earliest times as a magic potion—a charm
against restless ghosts. Whether you want some incense to settle
your own ghosts, to add ritual and mystery to your home or
merely to add aroma, there is nothing better than making your
own. The following recipes produce incense that will soothe and
relax you—and from a relaxed person comes inner beauty.

Traditionally there have been two ways to burn incense—loose and sprinkled onto glowing charcoal or blended with charcoal and gum and shaped into sticks or cones. The gummed incense needs a good draft to burn, which is why in churches the incense burner is swung backward and forward to produce a moving current of air to help the charcoal to glow.

Loose Incense

You will need:
- 🕯 1 oz (25 g) gum benzoin (from a pharmacist)
- 🕯 1 oz (25 g) powdered sandalwood
- 🕯 ¾ oz (20 g) ground cassia bark
- 🕯 ¾ oz (20 g) ground

cardamom seeds
- 🕯 ½ oz (15 g) ground cloves

Blend the ingredients together—you will find that the gum acts as a fixative. The cassia can be replaced with cinnamon; this is a basic recipe, so experiment.

Shaped Incense

You will need:
- 🕯 ¼ oz (10 g) powdered sandalwood
- 🕯 ¼ oz (10 g) ground cassia
- 🕯 3½ oz (100 g) gum arabic
- 🕯 1 oz (25 g) powdered gum benzoin
- 🕯 7 oz (200 g) charcoal

You need to crush the charcoal finely and add it to the dry ingredients. Mix the gum arabic with water to form a stiff paste, then stir in the rest of the ingredients. Form the incense into any shape you want and let dry for a day or two. Again you can use this basic recipe and add any other ingredients you like.

Remember that when burning incense, the fumes may be toxic, so make sure you have adequate ventilation.

PERFUME

Slice five vanilla beans and immerse in pure alcohol. Leave for six weeks but shake daily. At the end of this, strain the alcohol off, and you will have a pleasantly refreshing perfume.

POTPOURRI

A spicy potpourri will add a heavy, pungent scent to any room and give you an invigorating aroma. To make a dry potpourri, you can blend and grind any spices that you want—you can experiment and add spices as you try them in your cooking. A basic mixture would use rose petals as a base, or you could try crushed bay leaves. Then add to this base finely ground allspice, cassia, cinnamon, aniseed, nutmeg, vanilla bean, coriander seeds, cloves, ginger, cardamom and mace.

Here are two other combinations you might like to try:

A light, refreshing, spring-time potpourri mixture
You will need:
- 2 oz (50 g) caraway
- 2 oz (50 g) cardamom
- 2 oz (50 g) cinnamon
- 2 oz (50 g) fennel
- 2 marigold flowers
- 6 drops neroli essential oil
- 6 drops lemon grass essential oil

A rich potpourri mixture with an aroma of Christmas
You will need:

- 1 oz (25 g) cinnamon sticks
- 2 oz (50 g) cloves
- 2 oz (50 g) star anise
- 2 oz (50 g) juniper berries
- 2 oz (50 g) black pepper
- 2 oz (50 g) myrtle leaves
- 1 oz (25 g) rosemary
- 6 drops essential oil of frankincense
- 2 drops essential oil of cinnamon
- 6 drops essential oil of orange
- 2 drops essential oil of ginger

BEAUTY TREATMENTS
Hand Cream

You will need:

- 🌿 2 oz (60 g) vanilla beans
- 🌿 9 oz (250 g) pure lard
- 🌿 4 oz (120 g) gum benzoin
- 🌿 4 oz (120 g) spermaceti (from a pharmacist)
- 🌿 2 large cups (500 ml) almond oil

Put the vanilla beans and lard in a bowl with the gum benzoin, spermaceti and almond oil. Heat in a double boiler. Let cool and use as an all-over body lotion for massages. Aniseed makes a refreshing nerve tonic if a few drops of aniseed oil are added to the bath water—this is good for nervous headaches and tiredness. It is also good as a massage oil; add two drops of aniseed oil to two drops of nutmeg and rose and add this all to 1 tbsp of almond oil.

Other suitable essential oils of spices include: dill (for digestive problems and colic in children); fennel (for digestive problems); ginger (for nervous disorders); juniper (to help detoxify and cleanse); black pepper (to increase circulation); and lemongrass (for refreshment).

For a massage to aid digestion and colic, add 3 drops of essential oil of dill and 3 drops of essential oil of fennel to almond oil. For a refreshing and stimulating massage, add 1 drop essential oil of pepper and 3 drops of essential oil of lemongrass to 3⅓ tbsp (50 ml) of almond oil. Essential oils of spices are generally warming and stimulating and, if used too strongly, can be irritating to the skin. When using on someone with sensitive skin or with children, use half the recommended amount of essential oil.

CLEANSING LOTION AND AFTERSHAVE

Nutmeg: For a soothing and firming lotion for breasts, infuse ½ oz (15 g) of nutmeg in 4 cups (1 l) of boiling water. Strain and soak the cloths in the liquid and leave on the breasts until the cloths cool. Repeat by warming the liquid.

Horseradish has a use in skin care.

Horseradish: This spice makes a good cleansing lotion to get rid of pimples and blackheads. Slice the root and add to milk—9 oz (250 g) of root to 1 cup (250 ml) of milk—simmer over a low heat for one hour, then strain. Use the lotion on the face and forehead. Keep this bottled and in the refrigerator.

Coriander: This spice can be used to make a pleasant aftershave. Use 2 oz (60 g) of coriander seeds with 1 tsp (5 ml) of honey and 2 cups (½ l) of hot water. Let simmer for 20 minutes and cool. Add 1 tbsp (15 ml) of witch hazel and strain into a bottle. Keep the aftershave in the refrigerator, and it will be especially refreshing.

EYE LOTION

Fennel: For an eye lotion, simmer 2 oz (50 g) of crushed seeds in 2 cups (500 ml) of water for 30 minutes. Strain and let cool. Use this in an eye lotion using an eyebath to relieve inflammation.

HAIR PREPARATIONS

Clove: This makes an excellent preparation with a pleasant scent for hair. Heat 1 lb (½ kg) of benzoate lard with 1 cup (250 ml) of almond oil and 2 tbsp (30 ml) of palm oil. Strain and add, while still warm, 2 tbsp (30 ml) of eau de cologne and 1 tsp (5 ml) of oil of cloves.

Saffron used as a final rinse tints hair a rich goldon color.

Star Anise: This is used in another good preparation for hair. Crush and boil 120 g of seeds in a cup of water and add the resulting oil to olive oil—1 tsp (5 ml) of oil of star anise to 10 tsp (150 ml) of olive oil. This helps the growth of new hair.

Saffron: For tinting fair hair a rich golden color, soak one dash of saffron in 2 cups (½ l) of boiling water. Let cool. The saffron water can be used as a wash after shampooing. Do not rinse—leave the hair wet and allow to dry naturally.

🌿

ROUGE AND LIPSTICKS

Safflower: A gentle rouge can be made from safflower. Soak a handful of safflower flowers in 2 cups (½ l) of boiling water. When cool, you will have a red liquid to which you add three parts rice powder and one part kaolin until you have a smooth paste. A little applied as a rouge or lipstick adds color to a pale face.

BEAUTY SOAPS

Soap was first made and used in Rome nearly 3,000 years ago, and you can make your own spicy soaps quite simply.

Basic Soap

You will need:

- 9 oz (250 g) tallow
- 5 fl oz (150 ml) soft water
- 2 tbsp (30 ml) caustic soda
- dash of turmeric
- 1 tsp (5 g) ground caraway
- 1 tsp (5 g) ground sandalwood powder
- 1 ground clove
- 3 tsp (15 g) ground nutmeg
- 1 tbsp (15 ml) honey
- 1 tbsp (15 ml) olive oil

Melt the tallow in a pan. Pour the water into a separate pan and add the caustic soda. The caustic and water will react, causing heat, and you will have to allow it to cool down. Let the tallow also cool down. When both are lukewarm, pour the melted tallow and oil into the caustic soda and stir all the while—ideally use a whisk.

Add the dry ingredients (finely ground) and the honey and keep stirring. As you whisk you will suddenly find that your liquid turns into a thick, creamy paste. This is your soap. Turn it out into molds and let it set for 24 hours. Turn it out from the mold—by this time it will be quite hard—and leave it in a warm, well-ventilated cupboard for about two weeks. Then your spicy soap will be ready to use. It lathers easily and leaves your skin enriched and beautiful—and smelling aromatic and spicy.

This is a basic soap recipe—you can try experimenting and adding your own choice of spices. The turmeric adds yellow color—you might like to try paprika for a red tint or a little finely chopped parsley for green.

CAUTION

Caustic soda in its dry form will burn if it is allowed to come into contact with skin—wash it off with cold water immediately.

SPICES FOR HEALTH

In the thirteenth century Pope Innocent III passed an edict that no ecclesiastic should practice medicine for profit or shed blood in any way. Up until then all medical practitioners in Europe were in the holy orders. This edict meant that surgery passed into the hands of lay people, mostly barbers, while church priests and monks devoted their time to the search for cures based on natural plants. In effect, it meant that there was a considerable division between herbalists and surgeons—the latter in the holy orders concerned themselves more with the theoretical aspects of medicine. This led to an enormous upsurge in interest in plants that had an effect on a patient's condition. As the Spanish and Portuguese explorers came back from the New World with new plants and spices, these were seized on as being miraculous—and, in certain cases, as having far greater powers than they actually did. However, spices do have a natural

warming effect and are of some use against colds, coughs and flu symptoms. The following medicinal recipes should be taken only for the very mildest of conditions. Any illnesses that you would not normally treat at home should not be treated with spice remedies. Consult a qualified medical doctor if you are not sure.

Colds and Coughs

Spices are warming—and what could be better to ward off the effects of cold winter conditions?

Cayenne Pepper Tea: Stir ½ tsp (2½ ml) of cayenne pepper into 5 fl oz (150 ml) of boiling water. Let cool and sip slowly. This is said to ward off a cold before it has had a chance to take hold, and it will certainly warm your whole system. You can substitute hot milk for the water if you prefer.

Ginger and Honey Tea: Stir ½ tsp (2½ ml) of dried ginger powder into hot milk and add 1 tsp (5 ml) of honey. This is a warming drink to reduce the symptoms of a cold.

Cardamom Tea: To reduce the effects of a winter flu fever, mix 1 tsp (5 ml) of basil with the seeds of one large cardamom pod and ½ tsp (2½ ml) of ground cinnamon in 2 cups (500 ml) of boiling water with 1 tsp (5 ml) of sugar. Infuse

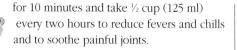

for 10 minutes and take ½ cup (125 ml) every two hours to reduce fevers and chills and to soothe painful joints.

Anise Tea: For soothing a cough and to loosen phlegm infuse 2 tsp (10 ml) of crushed aniseed in 1 cup (300 ml) of boiling water. Drink when cool.

SEDATIVES AND RELAXANTS

When we cannot sleep or we feel the need for something to relax us when we are stressed, spice teas are natural, nonaddictive ways to help us.

Fennel, Dill and Anise Tea: To make a relaxing drink before bed to help you sleep, take crushed seeds of fennel, anise and dill—1 tsp (5 ml) of each—in 1 cup (250 ml) of hot water.

TONIC

Eating any of the sweet peppers increases vitamin C intake, and you can make teas from other spices to provide a tonic to help strengthen the whole system.

Ginseng Tea: Add 1 tsp (5 ml) of powdered ginseng in 2 cups (500 ml) of boiling water. Simmer for 15 minutes and sip slowly when cool.

Caraway Tea: Take 1 tsp (5 ml) of caraway seeds in 1 cup (250 ml) of hot water.

Caper Tea: Take 1 tsp (5 ml) of dried and ground capers in 1 cup (250 ml) of hot water.

Celery Tea: Take 1 tsp (5 ml) of ground celery seeds in 1 cup (250 ml) of hot water.

Fenugreek Tea: Take 1 tsp (5 ml) of ground fenugreek seeds in 1 cup (250 ml) of hot water.

Digestive Tonics

After the winter, when all people had to eat were salty, stodgy foods, they needed a good digestive tonic to cleanse the system and restore a sluggish stomach.

Fenugreek Tea (recipe above): Make a tea as a general tonic, and you will find it will also increase appetite.

Spicy Brandy Tonic: Steep 1 tsp (5 ml) each of crushed fennel, aniseed and caraway seeds in 2½ cups (600 ml) of brandy with ¼ cup (50 g) sugar. Let mature for four weeks—shake occasionally. Strain. Take ½ cup (125 ml) before meals.

Bitter Brandy Tonic: Take this as an aperitif before meals to settle the stomach; if taken half an hour before eating, it stimulates the appetite. To 4 cups (1 l) of brandy add 2 tsp (30 ml) of dried orange peel; 2 tsp (10 ml) of crushed cardamom seeds, ½ tsp (2½ ml) of ground cinnamon; ¼ tsp (1 ml) of ground cloves. Bottle this and store it for a month. Take 2 tbsp (30 ml) before meals.

Nutmeg Wine: Take this as an aperitif half an hour before meals. Add one whole grated nutmeg to 2 cups (500 ml) of red wine. Allow to steep overnight. Strain. Take 2 tbsp (30 ml) before meals.

Juniper Berry Wine: Soak 1 tbsp (15 ml) of juniper berries in 4 cups (1 l) of white wine. Sweeten with 1 tbsp (15 ml) of brown sugar. Let mature for one week and then strain and drink a glass or two as required.

Syrup of Juniper Berries: Take this after meals to settle the stomach. Simmer 4 lb (100 g) of juniper berries, fresh or dried, and the peel of one lemon in 4 cups (1 l) of water until they soften. Strain, add 2 tbsp (30 ml) of honey, bring to a boil and simmer until the syrup thickens. You can bottle and use immediately. To keep fresh, keep in the refrigerator. Take 1 tbsp (15 ml) after meals.

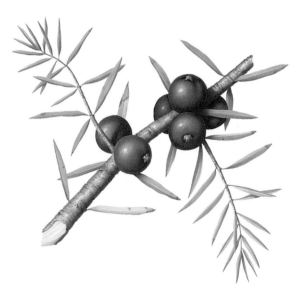

Ginger and Honey Mulled Wine: This is a good digestive tonic for those who suffer from winter chills or have poor appetites. Heat a little red wine, making sure the wine doesn't boil (or boil it for children if you want to get rid of the alcoholic content). Add some finely grated ginger according to taste and then leave to cool. Add honey—1 tsp to each glass.

Cinnamon Milk: This will act as a good digestive remedy. Take ½ tsp (2½ ml) of ground cinnamon in 1 cup (250 ml) of hot milk with a little honey added. This is good at night because it not only settles the stomach and cures indigestion, but it also induces sleep.

Cardamom Tea: Crush the seeds from one pod of cardamom and add to 1 cup (250 ml) of boiling water. Allow to cool and sip slowly. This relieves indigestion.

Digestive Teas: You can infuse the seeds of anise, cumin, coriander and caraway to make teas to settle upset stomachs. Any of these seeds can be infused in milk or can be chewed after meals. They also sweeten the breath.

Cardamom Coffee: In Arab countries this is called gahwa and is drunk hot and strong. It is considered so beneficial for settling digestion that you are not allowed to speak while the coffee-drinking ceremony is being carried out because it would only undo all the good work the coffee is doing. Crush green coffee beans and add crushed cardamom pods and seeds with a little ground clove (only a dash) to hot water and boil for two minutes. Strain and serve hot and black with sugar.

LAXATIVES

Either through poor eating habits or stress, we may sometimes experience constipation and laxatives may be necessary. Any long-term need for them should be referred to a qualified medical doctor.

Aniseed and Licorice Laxative: Soak 1 oz (25 g) of licorice root overnight with six dried figs or prunes—or both if you prefer. In the morning simmer with ½ tsp (2½ ml) of aniseed and 1 tsp (5 ml) of honey for 15 minutes. Remove the licorice and eat the fruit for breakfast.

BINDING AGENTS

Again, any long-term need for binding agents to ease or cure diarrhea should be checked with a doctor.

Allspice Binding Agent: Add ½ tsp (2½ ml) of crushed allspice berries to 4 cups (1 l) of water and 1 tbsp (15 ml) of bilberries (soaked overnight). Bring to a boil and simmer gently for a few minutes. Allow to cool and add 1 tsp (5 ml) of lemon juice. Stir. Take a cup every few hours until the symptoms pass.

RHEUMATISM REMEDIES

Cinnamon: To relieve the pain of rheumatic joints, add a few drops of oil of cinnamon to olive oil and massage into the affected area to bring relief. Likewise, you can gently heat juniper berries in olive oil for an hour and allow to cool and use as a pain-relieving massage oil. Inflamed or swollen joints should not be massaged.

Juniper Berries: These can be used in a tea and taken internally to relieve the pain of rheumatic joints.

TOOTHACHE REMEDY

Clove: To relieve toothache pain, simply clamp a whole clove to the painful tooth and leave for a while to relieve the pain—and then go straight to a dentist.

SPICES FOR ALL-AROUND HEALTH

Star Anise: This is a diuretic and appetite stimulant and is also useful for relieving flatulence and nausea.

Licorice: This reduces inflammation and spasms, expels phlegm and soothes the bronchials.

Elecampane: The warming qualities of elecampane make it a good expectorant and a treatment for bronchitis, asthma and other pulmonary infections.

Dill: This is rich in sulfur, potassium and sodium.

Celery: A poultice of the leaves of celery can be used externally for fungal infections, and the seeds taken in small quantities internally are good for relieving gout, arthritis and inflammation of the urinary tract.

Horseradish: This is a diuretic. It increases perspiration, which can be good for some fevers. It can be made into a poultice to be used externally for wound infections, arthritis and pleurisy.

Java Galangal: This is a warming digestive and is useful as a remedy for diarrhea, gastric upsets that are sensitive to cold and incontinence.

Galangal: This can be taken internally for chronic gastritis, digestive upsets, gastric ulcerations and to relieve the pain of rheumatism.

Mustard: This can be used in the form of mustard plasters, bandages soaked in mustard, and applied as a poultice to relieve rheumatism, muscular pain and chilblains. They can be used to soak feet for relief from aches and strains and also to cure headaches and colds; use cold water to maximize the heating effect. People with sensitive skin should take care because it can cause blistering. In large doses it causes vomiting.

Safflower: This can be taken as a tea and is good for coronary-artery disease and menopausal and menstruation problems.

Capers: These are used to revitalize and increase digestion and appetite. They are good for gastrointestinal infections and diarrhea.

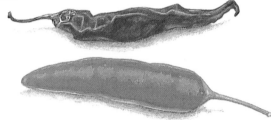

Chilies: These are revitalizing, help digestion and have a strong stimulant effect.

Cayenne: You can infuse cayenne to make a hot, fiery tea to stimulate the appetite and to relieve stomach and bowel pains and cramps.

Sweet Peppers: These contain large amounts of vitamin C. They also have revitalizing and antiseptic qualities and stimulate the digestive system.

Paprika: The warming qualities of paprika make it effective as a reliever of cold symptoms as well as a rich and valuable source of vitamin C.

Caraway: These seeds can be chewed for immediate relief of indigestion and colic as well as menstrual pains and cramps.

Grains of Paradise: The seeds are used internally in western Africa for a wide range of ailments including painful menstruation and excessive lactation.

Cassia: This is a major ingredient in cold remedies and is used for treating dyspepsia, flatulence and colic.

Cilantro: This is a useful remedy for minor digestive problems, and the coriander seeds can reduce the effects of some laxatives, which can produce painful stomach spasms.

Cumin: Minor digestive disorders may be helped if cumin is taken internally. It settles stomach upsets that cause migraines.

Turmeric: Taken internally, turmeric is good for digestive upsets and skin disorders.

Lemongrass: This can be taken internally by small children as a digestive aid. It can also be taken for mild fevers.

Cardamom: Taken internally, cardamom settles upset stomachs and counteracts the effects of dairy product allergies.

Cloves: Because they are a warming stimulant, cloves are useful for stimulating the digestive system. They can be taken internally for gastroenteritis and nausea, gastric upsets that are sensitive to cold, and impotence.

Asafetida: This cleans and restores the digestive tract and relieves stomach pains and colic.

Fennel: This relieves digestive disorders and reduces inflammation. It can be taken as a mouthwash and gargle for sore throats and ulcerated gums.

Juniper: This can be used for urinary tract infections—cystitis, urethritis and inflammation of the kidneys—as well as for gout and rheumatism.

Mace: This can be used to treat stomach disorders such as diarrhea, dysentery and indigestion.

Nutmeg: In small doses, nutmeg is a carminative, meaning it reduces flatulence and digestive discomfort. It is useful in treating flatulence and vomiting and for improving overall digestion.

Myrtle: This reduces colic, flatulence and digestive discomfort, is an expectorant and is helpful in all types of chest infections.

Nigella: These seeds are said to benefit digestion and reduce inflammation or irritation in the gut lining.

Opium Poppy: This is useful for treating cystitis and pyelitis.

Quassia: This is used to treat rheumatism and fevers as well as stomach disorders and dyspepsia.

Allspice: The oil of allspice is distilled and used for flatulent indigestion. It improves overall digestion and has a tonic effect on the nervous system.

Aniseed: The warming and stimulating properties of aniseed make it useful for treating circulation problems and digestive disorders.

Fenugreek: These seeds can be infused to treat gastric inflammation, colic, insufficient lactation, poor appetite and digestive disorders.

Cubeb: Because of its warming properties, cubeb will relieve coughs and bronchitis, sinusitis and throat infections.

Pepper: This is very good for stimulating the digestion, warming the bronchial passageways and relieving the congestion of colds and flu.

Sumac: This is sometimes prescribed herbally for treating severe diarrhea, and the root bark is used to treat dysentery. The fruits are used for treating urinary infections.

Sesame: These seeds are used as a mild and gentle laxative.

White Mustard: This is used to treat bronchial congestion, colds, coughs and rheumatic joint pains.

Tamarind: This makes an excellent laxative—its action is fairly gentle. It is also used to treat fevers, asthma, jaundice and dysentery.

Vanilla: This has few medicinal uses apart from aiding digestion and improving appetite.

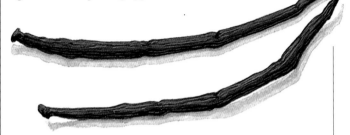

Ginger: Recent research has shown ginger to be excellent for settling the stomach, and it is now used as a travel sickness remedy.

Curry: The bark of the curry plant is used internally for digestive problems and the leaves are used as an infusion for constipation and colic.

Szechuan Pepper: This is a stimulant that works on the spleen and stomach. It also has properties that can lower blood pressure.

Saffron: You can infuse saffron to make an herbal tea that can be taken as a warming soothing drink to clear the head. It can also shake off drowsiness and bring on menstruation.

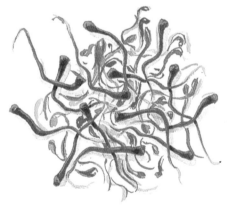

Cinnamon: This strong stimulant of the glandular system helps relieve stomach upsets. It is very warming, so it is good for relieving the symptoms of colds, flu and sore throats.

ADDITIONAL READING

Day, Avanelle and Lillie Stuckey. *The Spice Cookbook*. David White Company, 1964.

Gunst, Kathy. *Condiments*. G. P. Putnam & Sons, 1984.

Herbst, Sharon Tyler. *The New Food Lover's Companion*. New York: Barron's Educational Series, 1995.

Pratt, James Norwood. *The Tea Lover's Treasury*. 101 Productions, 1982.

Rain, Patricia. *Vanilla Cookbook*. Celestial Arts, 1986.

Schapira, Joel, David and Karl. *The Book of Coffee and Tea*. St. Martin's Press, 1975.

Sobart, Tom. *Herbs, Spices and Flavorings*. The Overlook Press, 1982.

Stone, Sally and Martin. *The Mustard Cookbook*. Avon Books, 1981.

Townsend, Doris McFerran. *Herbs, Spices & Flavorings*. HPBooks, 1982.

Westland, Pamela. *The Book of Spices*. New York: Exeter Books, 1985.

ACKNOWLEDGMENTS

The Publishers would like to thank Kay Quigley, Darren Braithwaite, and Liz Day of Schwartz, McCormick UK Ltd, Haddenham, Buckinghamshire, England for advice and help in the supply of the vast majority of spices photographed for this book. We would also like to thank Joseph Flach of Peterborough, England, and Fox's Spices of Stratford upon Avon, Warwickshire, England, for advice and the supply of some of the more unusual spices (Fox's Spices are available by mail order on Tel: (00 44) 1789 266420, Fax: (00 44) 1789 267737.

The author would like to thank Roni Jay for her help with the research for this book and all the wonderful explorers, cooks, chefs, cookery writers and spice merchants who have gone before and fired my imagination about spices.

PICTURE CREDITS

INDEX

Index

Index